intimate
GATHERINGS

great food *for* good friends

intimate
GATHERINGS

great food *for* good friends

Ellen Rose and Jessica Strand

Photographs by Maura McEvoy

CHRONICLE BOOKS

SAN FRANCISCO

Acknowledgments

We would like to thank *Juli Tantum* for her invaluable help and input. We are also indebted to our enthusiastic tasters and testers, *Jasmin Aquirre, Stacy Hunt, Tracy Scott,* and *Bruce Miller.* A special thanks to *Tim Fischer,* who kept The Cook's Library running beautifully while we were in the kitchen, and for his thoughts, suggestions, and willingness to try any of our menu items. And of course, all of our dinner party guests over the past year who willingly sampled and commented on our many creations. And, last but not least, the folks at Chronicle Books who helped make our book a reality. Especially *Leslie Jonath,* our editor, who shepherded our first book through the process of publishing with advice and support, *Suzanne Sherman* who meticulously edited our manuscript, and *Maura McEvoy* for being the eyes to our creations with her beautiful photography.

Text copyright © 1998 by Ellen Rose and Jessica Strand.
Photographs copyright © 1998 by Maura McEvoy. All rights reserved. No part of this book may be reproduced in any form without written permission from the publisher.

Library of Congress Cataloging-in-Publication Data:

Rose, Ellen
  Intimate gatherings: great food for good friends/
  by Ellen Rose and Jessica Strand;
  photographs by Maura McEvoy.
  p. cm.
  Includes Index
  ISBN 0-8118-1575-7
  1. Entertaining. 2. Cookery. 3. Menus.
  I. Strand, Jessica. II. Title.
  TX731.R59 1998
  642'.4—dc21   97-34150 CIP

Designed by Nina J. Miller.
Food styling by Roscoe Betsill.
Prop styling by Maura McEvoy and Marlene Niehaus.
The photographer wishes to thank
Christopher, Jim, John, and Willis for providing
an inspirational setting.

Printed in Hong Kong.

Distributed in Canada by Raincoast Books
8680 Cambie Street
Vancouver, British Columbia V6P 6M9

10 9 8 7 6 5 4 3 2

Chronicle Books
85 Second Street
San Francisco, California 94105

www.chroniclebooks.com

♦

To our
most
intimate
eaters,

DEDICATION

Bob, Molly, Jason

&

Stephen.

♦

C · O · N · T

❧ *Fall*

Dinner for Two *72*

MENU MANAGER *73*
Hot and Spicy Flavored Nuts
Rapini with Garlic and Olive Oil
Pork Tenderloin with Fall Fruits in a
    Reduced Port Sauce
Perfect Mashed Potatoes
Sautéed Caramelized Apple Slices with
    Cinnamon Ice Cream

Dinner for Four *80*

MENU MANAGER *81*
Crostini with Two Toppings
Fennel, Mascarpone, and Fresh Herb Risotto
Mixed Green Salad with
    Elizabeth's Parmesan Wafers
Autumn Mixed Nut Tart

Dinner for Six *90*

MENU MANAGER *91*
Cured Salmon with Thinly Sliced Fennel
Wide Noodles with Mussels in Mustard Cream
    with Leeks, Peas, and Tarragon
Baby Spinach with French Feta, Walnuts, and
    Roasted Red Bell Peppers
Roasted Fall Figs with Brown Sugar Crust and
    Crème Fraîche

❧ *Winter*

Dinner for Two *102*

MENU MANAGER *103*
Lamb Chops on Garlicky Winter Greens
Cheesy Potato Gratin
Endive, Apple, Blue Cheese, and Hickory Nut Salad
Stephen's Cherry Biscotti

Dinner for Four *110*

MENU MANAGER *111*
Bob's Classic Martini with Caperberries
Cheese Torta
Fennel Soup with Roasted Garlic Croutons
Bistro Skillet Steak with Reduced Burgundy Sauce
Hot Potato and Frisee Salad
Caramelized Banana Bread Pudding

Dinner for Six *120*

MENU MANAGER *121*
Winter Sangria
Fruity Fig and Black Olive Spread
Winter Pot Roast with Juniper Berries
Caramelized Root Vegetables
Chopped Winter Greens with Candied Pecans
    and Honey Dressing
Fresh Gingery Gingerbread

Introduction

The point of most small gatherings is to share and enjoy the company of others. And with everyone's busy lives, what could be nicer than having a home-cooked meal with close friends or family? It is with this thought that we wrote *Intimate Gatherings*, simple, elegant menus for small gatherings.

When you think of an intimate gathering, what comes to mind? Perhaps a summer evening picnic on the beach, or maybe *romantic* dinner for two in front of the fire on a frosty winter's night. In fall it might be a birthday party with family in the dining room; in springtime, a lunch with a couple of friends on the patio or terrace.

Moods change with the seasons and so do the places we eat and the foods we serve. In spring you shed your winter coat and leave behind the heavy foods of winter. Foods like baby peas, asparagus, and strawberries are readily available. When you invite people over to share a meal, you leave windows open, excited by the warming temperatures. Summer's long hours of light and hot weather invite you to spend as much time outside as possible. Summer brings a wide variety of *luscious* produce—ripe tomatoes, berries, peaches, cherries. When you have friends over, you light the grill and eat your meal on the balcony. In the fall the smells of fallen leaves and fires burning begin to fill the air. We tend to eat earlier and want to eat more. The season brings crispy apples, pears, figs, and a craving for hearty foods. Winter forces us back indoors where we settle in for the season. We yearn for *rich*, warm roasts and other comfort foods.

The recipes in *Intimate Gatherings* are arranged by season. Each section includes menus for gatherings of two, four, or six people. (The recipes can always be doubled for larger gatherings, if needed.) In dividing menus by season, we focus on the *tastiest* foods that are fresh and accessible. Preceding each section you'll find a helpful step-by-step preparation plan designed to help you plan your dinner from beginning to end so you'll have time to spend with your guests and you won't be a slave to your kitchen.

❖

The recipes combine our versions of some American classics with recipes influenced by Italian, French, and Mediterranean cuisines. We have aimed to make every stage—from the buying of the food, to its preparation, to finally serving the meal—as enjoyable as possible. We feel strongly that no matter how small the gathering, it should always be special and *fun*. We hope *Intimate Gatherings* will provide an anxiety-free, enjoyable, appetizing approach toward dinners with your family and friends.

———◆———

S · P · R

When spring arrives, we enjoy the abundance of new life around us. We emerge from our winter hibernation, opening windows and doors, ready to share the pleasures of the new season with close friends. Spring is about enjoying the warming temperatures, the blooming flowers and fruit trees, and the young, flavorful foods—what could be better than enjoying the season's bounty with friends and family?

In spring we attend farmers' markets, where we find the variety of fresh, young produce wonderfully overwhelming. Our Braised Roman-Style Artichokes, Oven-Roasted Asparagus with Parmesan, Market Pea Soup with Lettuce, Mixed Florentine Bean Salad, and Strawberries with Amaretti Topping all take advantage of the season and are simple to prepare.

Spring also signals the return of fresh seafood. We've included Crispy-Skin Salmon on a Bed of Spring Greens as well as the Italian seafood soup, cioppino, which contains clams, mussels, shrimp, sea bass, and whatever other fish is fresh at your fish market.

We've included two desserts that incorporate the best of spring: blood oranges and strawberries. The blood oranges are used in a refreshing and cool sorbet, and the strawberries are combined with the smooth taste of a hearty red wine to create a perfect finish to a meal.

I · N · G

DINNER FOR

2

Radishes and a Mélange of Baby Spring Vegetables with Herb Sauce

◆

Market Pea Soup with Lettuce

◆

Crispy-Skin Salmon on a Bed of Spring Greens

◆

Roasted Baby New Potatoes with a Fistful of Herbs

◆

Spiked Blood Orange Sorbet

Menu Manager

1 day before dinner: **1.** Prepare Spiked Blood Orange Sorbet

Day of dinner: **1.** Prepare vegetables and Herb Sauce
2. Prepare Market Pea Soup with Lettuce

About 1 hour before serving: **1.** Preheat the oven to 425 degrees
2. Prepare Roasted Baby New Potatoes and bake

30 minutes before serving: **1.** Slowly reheat the soup
2. Prepare Crispy-Skin Salmon and the spring greens

Just before serving: **1.** Put sorbet in refrigerator to soften

❃ Radishes and a Mélange of **Baby Spring Vegetables** with Herb Sauce

Serves 2

Herb sauces are found in almost every cuisine. Ours is a light, refreshing sauce which is great as a snack with fresh vegetables or as a sauce for meat, fish, or cooked vegetables.

Herb Sauce

3 tablespoons olive oil
1 tablespoon red wine vinegar
1 shallot, finely chopped
1 tablespoon finely chopped fresh basil
2 teaspoons finely chopped fresh tarragon
1 tablespoon finely chopped fresh mint
2 tablespoons finely chopped fresh Italian parsley
1 anchovy fillet, minced
1 clove garlic, minced
Salt and freshly ground black pepper, to taste

10 radishes
4 baby zucchini
4 baby yellow squash
8 thin asparagus, ½ inch removed from ends

1. Pour the oil and vinegar into a medium mixing bowl and whisk until combined. Add the remaining ingredients for the herb sauce and continue whisking for another 1 or 2 minutes, until the sauce is completely blended. Season with salt and pepper.

2. Arrange the vegetables on a platter with the herb sauce pooled in the center, and serve.

Market Pea Soup with Lettuce

Serves 2

This recipe requires just enough shelling for two people to handle easily. The traditional French method of combining baby lettuce with spring peas creates a very fresh, delicate soup.

1 tablespoon unsalted butter
1 tablespoon olive oil
1 medium leek, white part only, coarsely chopped
1 small head boston lettuce, coarsely chopped (3 cups)
¼ cup coarsely chopped Italian parsley
2 cups chicken stock
1 cup fresh or frozen green peas (thawed)
Salt and freshly ground black pepper, to taste
¼ cup half-and-half, optional

1. Melt the butter with the olive oil in a medium saucepan over medium-low heat. Add the leeks to the pan and cook until the leeks are soft, 7 to 10 minutes.

2. Add the lettuce and the parsley to the pan and cook, stirring constantly, for 1 to 2 minutes, until wilted. Add the chicken stock and peas. Bring to a boil, then reduce heat to low and simmer, uncovered, for 10 minutes.

3. Remove the soup from the stove. Use an electric or a hand-held blender to puree the soup in batches until smooth. Return soup to a clean pan over low heat. Season with salt and pepper. Stir in the half-and-half, if using, and heat until warmed through. Do not boil. Adjust the seasonings to taste.

4. Ladle the warm soup into bowls and serve immediately.

✿ Crispy-Skin **Salmon** on a Bed of **Spring Greens**

Serves 2

Sweet, buttery salmon accented with the earthy, peppery taste of spring greens is a delicious combination. We recommend cooking the salmon in a cast-iron skillet, but feel free to grill it if you prefer; both methods give the fish a smokiness and crispiness that contrasts well with the fresh, clean taste of the greens. It is important to note that a regular or nonstick frying pan is not recommended as it will not allow the salmon filet to crisp the way that a cast-iron skillet or grill can.

6 tablespoons olive oil

1 large clove garlic, minced

1 bunch beet greens, rinsed well, center red stems removed, and cut in thirds crosswise

1 bunch mustard greens, rinsed well, stems removed, and leaves cut in half crosswise

2 bunches baby spinach, rinsed well (if larger spinach leaves are used, remove stems and chop leaves crosswise)

2 tablespoons freshly squeezed lemon juice

½ teaspoon salt, plus more, to taste

½ teaspoon pepper, plus more, to taste

2 salmon fillets (about 8 ounces each)

1. Heat 3 tablespoons of the olive oil in a medium saucepan over medium heat for about 2 minutes. Place the minced garlic into the saucepan and let it brown for 2 to 3 minutes. This will infuse the olive oil with garlic flavor. Remove the pan from the heat and discard the garlic.

2. Let the pan with the garlic-infused oil cool for several minutes, and then add the beet and mustard greens and the spinach. Heat over medium-low heat. Push the wilting greens down into the pan and sprinkle the lemon juice over the top. Turn the greens and cover for 3 to 4 minutes, or until all of the leaves are limp. Check to make sure greens are not sticking to the pan. If they are sticking, add 1 tablespoon water and stir gently. Add the salt and pepper and turn off the heat.

3. Rub 1 tablespoon of the olive oil into the skin of the washed and dried salmon filets. Pour the remaining olive oil into a cast-iron skillet. The olive oil should just cover the bottom of the pan. Heat the oil over medium heat until hot. Test it by sprinkling a drop of water on the skillet; it should sizzle away in seconds. Place the salmon skin side down in the skillet and cook for 8 to 9 minutes. Check for doneness by gently pulling the flesh apart with a fork. It should flake easily and be a light orange in color. If the salmon is still bright orange and cold to the touch, cover with a lid and cook for 3 to 4 minutes, or until done.

4. Meanwhile, heat the greens again over very low heat, turning them occasionally. If there is excess liquid (more than 3 tablespoons), drain some of it. Place the greens on two plates and lay the fish fillets partially across them. Season with salt and pepper and serve.

✿ Roasted Baby **New Potatoes** with a Fistful of Herbs

Serves 2

These crisp baby new potatoes are great with fish, meat, or by themselves. They're a cross between a baked potato and a potato chip. What could be better?

1½ pounds baby new potatoes, scrubbed and quartered
2 tablespoons olive oil
½ teaspoon salt
½ teaspoon pepper
1½ teaspoons chopped fresh Italian parsley
1 teaspoon chopped fresh rosemary
1 teaspoon chopped fresh oregano
1 teaspoon minced fresh chives

1. Preheat the oven to 425 degrees.

2. Place the new potatoes in a large bowl and drizzle them with the olive oil. Add the salt, pepper, and herbs and toss.

3. Place the potatoes on a baking sheet, making sure that none of the potatoes are touching. (This helps them become crispy since the heat can only sear the exposed sides.)

4. Roast the potatoes in the oven for 20 minutes. Turn the potatoes with a metal spatula, making sure that all sides are becoming crisp. Roast for another 20 minutes. The potatoes should be browned on all sides and a fork should easily pierce their flesh.

5. Place the potatoes in a shallow bowl, and serve.

Spiked Blood Orange Sorbet

Serves 2

Adding vodka to this sorbet brings out the unique flavor of blood oranges for a refreshing, tangy, and colorful dessert. Be careful not to add too much vodka or the sorbet won't freeze properly.

¼ cup honey
Juice of 5 blood oranges (about 1¼ cups)
2 tablespoons vodka
Fresh mint leaves, for garnish

1. Heat the honey in a small saucepan over low heat. Swirl the pan gently until the honey liquefies, about 3 minutes. Remove from the heat and stir in ¼ cup of the blood orange juice. Put the remaining blood orange juice in a medium bowl. Stir the honey mixture into the blood orange juice, add the vodka, and stir well. Place the mixture in the refrigerator for several hours, or overnight.

2. Freeze the chilled mixture in an ice cream maker according to the manufacturer's instructions.

3. To serve, spoon the sorbet into chilled dishes and garnish with mint leaves.

DINNER FOR 4

Italian White Bean, Nut, and Herb Dip

◆

Marinated Olives

◆

Antonia's Cioppino

◆

Oven-Roasted Asparagus with Parmesan

◆

Strawberries with Amaretti Topping

Menu Manager

Several days before dinner: **1.** Prepare Marinated Olives

Day of dinner: **1.** Prepare strawberries and place in individual bowls, but do not add amaretti cookies until ready to serve
2. Prepare dip
3. Toast bread for cioppino

About 1 hour before serving: **1.** Preheat the oven to 425 degrees for Oven-Roasted Asparagus with Parmesan
2. Prepare Antonia's Cioppino

About 10 minutes before serving: **1.** Roast the asparagus and add the Parmesan

❁ Italian White Bean, Nut, and Herb **Dip**

Serves 4

This Italian-influenced dip is wonderful served with red and yellow peppers, endive, or toasted pita triangles. The mellow creaminess of the white beans gets a boost of flavor from the combination of herbs and garlic. If you have leftovers, it makes a terrific spread for a sandwich the next day.

1 tablespoon pine nuts
1 clove garlic, chopped
2 tablespoons chopped fresh basil
2 tablespoons chopped fresh Italian parsley
2 tablespoons chopped fresh tarragon
2 tablespoons chopped walnuts
½ teaspoon cayenne pepper
Juice of ½ lemon
3 tablespoons olive oil
½ teaspoon salt
½ (15-ounce) can cannelini beans
Basil leaves, for garnish
Italian parsley, for garnish

1. Preheat the oven to 400 degrees. Place the pine nuts in a pie tin and toast in the oven for 8 minutes, or until golden brown.

2. Puree all of the ingredients except the cannelini beans in a food processor or a blender. Add the cannelini beans and blend until smooth.

3. Spoon the dip into a serving bowl. Garnish with a few leaves of basil and Italian parsley.

❀ Marinated **Olives**

Serves 4

These olives should be made a couple of days ahead so that the flavors of the marinade can penetrate the olives. The olives are good to have around for a snack or to serve with a glass of wine when that unexpected guest arrives. If you become as crazy about them as Jessica is, you may even eat through a whole bowl by yourself in one sitting!

1 cup kalamata olives
1 cup gaeta olives
1 cup medium green olives
4 to 6 cloves garlic
2 tablespoons fennel seeds
2 to 3 small dried red chilies
2 bay leaves
1 cup olive oil

1. Strain the olives and place them in a large container with a tight-fitting lid. Add the garlic, fennel seeds, dried red chilies, bay leaves, and olive oil. Put the cover on the container and shake a few times. Let sit, covered, for 1 to 2 hours.

2. Shake the container a couple of times and refrigerate. The olives will keep for up to 2 months stored in the refrigerator.

♣ Antonia's **Cioppino**

Serves 4

Jessica's mother, Antonia, makes this delectable version of cioppino.
This much-loved Italian seafood soup is both simple to prepare and bursting
with flavor. Feel free to use any meaty fish available, with the exception of
bluefish or mackerel, which are too oily for the soup.

2 tablespoons olive oil
2 to 3 cloves garlic, minced, plus 1 whole clove
1 onion (Vidalia if available), chopped
3 leeks, chopped
½ carrot, diced
2 ribs celery, finely chopped
1 small Anaheim chili, seeded and finely chopped
12 to 15 canned plum tomatoes, quartered
3 to 4 (8-ounce) bottles clam juice
2½ cups water
1 cup dry white wine
1 teaspoon coarsely chopped fresh tarragon
1 teaspoon coarsely chopped fresh Italian parsley
1 teaspoon coarsely chopped fresh thyme
1 to 2 tablespoons Italian tomato paste (from the tube)
½ dozen clams, washed and soaked
½ dozen black mussels, debearded and scrubbed
1 pound sea bass, cut into 2-inch pieces
½ pound shark, cut into 2-inch pieces
8 jumbo shrimp, shelled and deveined
Salt and freshly ground pepper to taste
½ loaf French baguette, sliced and toasted

1. In a large stockpot over medium heat, add the olive oil, minced garlic, onion, leeks, carrot, celery, and chili. Sauté the vegetables for 10 minutes, or until soft. Add the tomatoes and cook for another 10 minutes. Add the clam juice, 2 cups of the water, wine, herbs, and tomato paste. Let simmer.

2. Place the clams and mussels and the remaining ½ cup water in a medium saucepan. Cover tightly and steam the mollusks over medium heat until they open, about 5 to 7 minutes. Turn off the heat.

3. Add the sea bass and shark to the large stockpot and cook for 3 to 4 minutes in the simmering broth. Add the shrimp and cook for another 4 minutes.

4. Strain the mollusk broth over cheesecloth or a fine-mesh strainer into a large bowl, making sure to eliminate any sand from the broth. Add the strained broth and the mollusks to the stockpot.

5. Slice the baguette into rounds. Drizzle the bread with olive oil and toast about 2 to 3 minutes, or until golden. Rub the toasted bread with the clove of garlic which has been halved. Place 2 to 3 bread rounds in the bottom of the bowl, and ladle cioppino over them. Serve immediately.

✿ Oven-Roasted **Asparagus** With Parmesan

Serves 4

The lemon dressing on the asparagus is a perfect complement to the fish soup. This method of cooking asparagus leaves its texture and distinctive flavor intact.

1 pound thin asparagus, ½ inch removed from ends
3 tablespoons olive oil, plus more for drizzling over asparagus
4 teaspoons freshly squeezed lemon juice
4 chopped anchovy fillets, or 1 tablespoon anchovy paste
2 tablespoons capers
Freshly grated Parmesan cheese
Salt and freshly ground black pepper, to taste

1. Preheat the oven to 425 degrees.

2. Place the asparagus in a shallow baking dish in a single layer.

3. Put the olive oil in a medium bowl. Add the lemon juice and chopped anchovies and whisk the mixture together. Add the capers and pour over the asparagus. Roll the asparagus in the dressing so that each spear is coated.

4. Place the baking dish on the center rack of the oven and roast for 8 minutes. Turn the asparagus over with a spoon and cook for another 4 minutes.

5. Keep the asparagus in the baking dish or transfer to a serving dish. Sprinkle the Parmesan cheese over the top, drizzle with olive oil, and season with salt and pepper. Spoon the sauce over the asparagus and serve.

Strawberries with Amaretti Topping

Serves 4

When strawberries appear in the markets, we know spring has arrived. This is a festive and simple finish to any meal, and the crunch of the amaretti cookies (Italian macaroons) makes it especially satisfying.

2 cups red wine (Zinfandel or Beaujolais)
¼ to ½ cup sugar
2 cups strawberries, stemmed and quartered (or cut in half, if small)
8 amaretti cookies, crumbled

1. Several hours before serving, combine the wine and sugar in a medium bowl. Add the strawberries and gently stir. Cover and refrigerate.

2. To serve, spoon the strawberries into individual bowls and pass the crumbled cookies in a separate bowl to top the fresh strawberries.

DINNER FOR

6

Braised Roman-Style Artichokes

◆

*Lamb Marinated in Lemon and Garlic
with Mint Pesto*

◆

Mixed Florentine Bean Salad

◆

Chocolate Pot de Crème

Menu Manager

1 day before dinner: **1.** Prepare Chocolate Pot de Crème and refrigerate

   2. Prepare marinade for lamb and marinate lamb overnight, turning several times

Day of dinner: **1.** Prepare artichokes; do not refrigerate

   2. Prepare Mixed Florentine Bean Salad

About 2 hours before serving: **1.** Bring lamb to room temperature

   2. Preheat the oven to 350 degrees for lamb

1½ hours before serving: **1.** Put lamb in oven to roast

   2. Prepare Mint Pesto

   3. Prepare flavored whipped cream

✤ Braised Roman-Style **Artichokes**

Serves 6

The term "braising" is used very loosely here. The artichokes are, in fact, steamed, but they have been doused with olive oil, vinegar, lemon, garlic, and herbs, which creates the effect of braising. The artichokes become so tender and flavorful no dipping sauce is needed.

6 globe artichokes
¼ cup plus 4 tablespoons olive oil
4 teaspoons cider vinegar
4 cloves garlic, minced
1 tablespoon chopped fresh oregano, or ½ teaspoon dried
1 tablespoon fresh chopped thyme, or 1 teaspoon dried
1 tablespoon fresh chopped rosemary, or ½ teaspoon dried
1 tablespoon fresh chopped mint
1 tablespoon chopped Italian parsley
Juice of 1 lemon
Salt and freshly ground black pepper, to taste

1. To prepare the artichokes: Cut off the tops and stems so the artichokes sit perfectly flat. Tear the first three rows of leaves off the base of the artichoke. Snip the thorns off the tips of the leaves.

2. Place a steamer filled with water over medium heat. Put the artichokes, leaves pointed up, into the steamer, so they fit snugly. Whisk together the ¼ cup olive oil and the vinegar in a small bowl and drizzle over. Mix together the garlic and herbs in a small bowl and sprinkle the mixture evenly. Sprinkle each artichoke with the lemon juice, salt, and pepper. Cover with a tight-fitting lid and cook for 35 minutes, or until done. Check for doneness by pulling a leaf out; if the leaf comes out easily with the meat intact, the artichokes are done.

3. To serve, place the artichokes in a serving dish and drizzle them with the 4 tablespoons olive oil. Spoon some of the marinade over each artichoke and season with salt and pepper.

Lamb Marinated in Lemon and Garlic with Mint Pesto

Serves 6

This flavorful fresh mint-based marinade makes the lamb even more tender and gives it a tangy garlic-citrus bite. The Mint Pesto can also be used to top such vegetables as string beans, artichokes, potatoes, or braised cabbage. Feel free to add more mint to the recipe if you like an even more vivid mint flavor.

Marinade

½ cup olive oil
4 cloves garlic, peeled
⅓ cup freshly squeezed lemon juice
Grated lemon zest of 1 lemon
¾ cup fresh mint leaves
Salt and freshly ground black pepper, to taste

1 (5-pound) leg of lamb, boned, butterflied, and trimmed of fat

Mint Pesto

3 cloves garlic, unpeeled
1 cup fresh mint leaves, or more, to taste
1 cup fresh Italian parsley
2 tablespoons balsamic vinegar
¼ teaspoon sugar
½ cup olive oil
Salt and freshly ground black pepper, to taste

Fresh mint sprigs, for garnish

1. To make the marinade: Combine all of the ingredients in a food processor or with a mortar and pestle.

2. Place the lamb in a shallow baking dish and spread the marinade on all surfaces of the lamb. Cover with plastic wrap, place in the refrigerator, and marinate for at least 4 hours, or overnight.

3. Take the lamb out of the refrigerator and bring it to room temperature (about 30 minutes).

4. Preheat the oven to 350 degrees.

5. Remove the lamb from the marinade. Reserve any of the marinade clinging to the meat. Roll the lamb up, beginning at the long end, and tie at 2-inch intervals with kitchen twine. Put the lamb in a shallow baking pan large enough to comfortably hold it and baste with remaining marinade. Roast for about 1½ hours. Test the internal temperature with a cooking thermometer. The thermometer should register 140 degrees for rare, 150 degrees for medium. Remove the lamb from the oven and let it sit for 20 minutes before carving.

6. Meanwhile, make the Mint Pesto. Put the 3 garlic cloves in a pie tin and roast for 15 minutes. Peel the roasted garlic and combine with other pesto ingredients in a blender or a food processor. Pulse the mixture several times. Season with salt and pepper.

7. To serve, slice the lamb into ½-inch slices and place on a serving dish. Garnish with mint sprigs. Serve sauce separately.

✤ Mixed Florentine **Bean Salad**

Serves 6

This spring salad is wonderful prepared several hours ahead and served at room temperature. Mix yellow beans with the green beans for a colorful dish.

½ cup blanched whole almonds

2 pounds green beans (or a combination
   of different varieties), trimmed

Croutons

6 (½-inch thick) slices Italian
   or French bread

3 tablespoons plus ¼ cup
   virgin olive oil

2 large cloves garlic, halved

Dressing

¼ cup raspberry vinegar

2 teaspoons Dijon mustard

1 tablespoon finely chopped lemon zest

Salt and freshly ground black pepper, to taste

½ cup thinly sliced red onion

¼ cup mixed chopped fresh herbs, such as
   basil, thyme, chives, and dill

½ cup crumbled goat cheese

1. Preheat the oven to 325 degrees.

2. Spread the almonds on a baking sheet and toast until golden, 5 to 8 minutes. Set aside to cool.

3. Bring a large saucepan of salted water to a boil. Add the beans and cook over medium heat until tender, 5 to 8 minutes. Drain beans and rinse with cold water. Drain well and set aside.

4. To make the croutons: Brush the bread with olive oil and toast in the oven until lightly golden. Rub the cut garlic on the bread. Cut or tear the bread into large cubes and set aside.

5. To make the dressing, whisk together the remaining ¼ cup olive oil, vinegar, mustard, lemon zest, salt, and pepper.

6. Place the green beans, red onion, tomatoes, herbs, and goat cheese in a large salad bowl and toss lightly, adding only a few tablespoons of dressing at a time so the dressing just coats the ingredients. Sprinkle the almonds and croutons on top and toss to mix. Cover dressed salad and let it rest at room temperature for all the flavors to meld.

Chocolate Pot de Crème

Serves 6

These lovely individual desserts are ideal served with a cup of hot coffee.

2 ounces milk chocolate
3 ounces bittersweet chocolate
1 cup heavy whipping cream
1 cup milk
½ cup sugar

3 large eggs plus 3 large egg yolks
1 tablespoon vanilla extract
2½ tablespoons Kahlùa
1 cup heavy whipping cream
1 tablespoon confectioners' sugar

1. Preheat the oven to 350 degrees. In a double boiler, melt the chocolate over simmering water. Set aside.

2. In a heavy saucepan, combine the cream, milk, and ¼ cup of the sugar. Heat just below the boiling point.

3. In a large bowl, beat the eggs, yolks and remaining ¼ cup sugar. Gradually add about ½ cup of the cream mixture, whisking continually. Add the remaining cream mixture and whisk until well combined. Add the vanilla extract and 1 tablespoon of the Kahlùa and stir until well combined. Let the mixture stand for 15 minutes.

4. Strain the mixture through a fine-mesh strainer into a bowl and then spoon into 6 pot de crème or custard cups. Place the cups in a deep pan and fill the pan halfway with hot water. Cover loosely with aluminum foil. Carefully place the pan in the oven and bake for 45 minutes, or until a knife inserted into the center comes out clean. If necessary, bake for 5 to 10 minutes more, checking after 2 minutes. Do not overbake.

5. Remove the custard cups from the water bath and set aside to cool. When cool, cover with plastic wrap, placing it directly on top of the chocolate. Refrigerate for 4 to 6 hours.

6. In a medium mixing bowl, beat the whipping cream for about 30 seconds. Add the sugar and the remaining 1½ tablespoons of Kahlùa and beat until soft peaks form. Store in a covered container in the refrigerator until ready to serve. Serve chilled, garnished with the whipped cream.

S · U · M

In summer, the most relaxing season, we allow ourselves time to lounge around, time to unwind. With so many hours of daylight, the days feel less confining. People eat later than at other times of year, and light, flavorful meals are more appealing than the comfort foods of fall and winter.

Wherever people live, whether in urban or rural areas, they like to spend the evening outside on the balcony, deck, or rooftop, or in the backyard. Summer brings to mind the fragrant aroma of food grilling as barbecues fire up around the neighborhood. When a friend drops by, what could be easier than grilling a couple of tuna steaks for a light meal? For a group of six, grilling two whole flattened chickens is festive. Our version has become a staple in our summer dinner party menus.

Having a small group over for dinner makes for a pleasant, casual evening. People are able to really talk with each other in a small group. Many of the foods on these summer menus create a social atmosphere—sharing barbecued mussels, slicing a tomato tart, dipping shrimp in the communal aioli sauce.

This season's menus are filled with summer's bounty. Inspired by the abundance of summer vegetables, our summer menu for four is completely vegetarian. Vegetable substitutions are possible in some cases, if you have a hankering for some particularly spectacular local produce, for example, and many of the fruits are interchangeable with other fruits; suggestions are noted in some of the recipes.

M · E · R

DINNER FOR

2

Barbecued Mussels in the Shell

♦

Grilled Tuna with Summer Nectarine Salsa

♦

Roasted Corn Salad with Avocado Vinaigrette

♦

*Homemade Yogurt Cheese with
Marinated Cherries*

Menu Manager

<table>
<tr><td>Up to 4 days before dinner:</td><td>1. Make yogurt cheese</td></tr>
<tr><td>Up to 1 day before dinner:</td><td>1. Prepare Summer Nectarine Salsa</td></tr>
<tr><td>Day of dinner:</td><td>1. Prepare Roasted Corn Salad with Avocado Vinaigrette, but do not add avocado
2. Prepare Marinated Cherries</td></tr>
<tr><td>1 hour before serving:</td><td>1. Heat grill to medium
2. Scrub and debeard mussels</td></tr>
<tr><td>About 15 minutes before serving:</td><td>1. Make Barbecued Mussels in the Shell and serve as appetizer
2. Put tuna on grill
3. Slice avocado and place on top of Roasted Corn Salad</td></tr>
<tr><td>After dinner:</td><td>1. Place yogurt cheese in individual bowls and spoon cherries and sauce over each serving</td></tr>
</table>

Barbecued **Mussels** in the Shell

Serves 2

These plump, smoky tidbits are perfect for two with a glass of white wine on a hot summer night. After removing the mussels from the grill, put the tuna on to cook, and enjoy these sumptuous little packages with a friend.

1 pound fresh mussels, debearded and scrubbed
½ cup dry white wine

1. Heat the grill.

2. Place the cleaned mussels evenly on the rack. Cover for 2 to 3 minutes, or until mussels begin to open. As they open, use tongs to turn the mussels so that the shell that the meat is attached to is closest to the flame.

3. Using a turkey baster, squirt a small amount of wine onto the meat of each mussel. Cook for another 1 to 2 minutes. Serve immediately from the grill.

Grilled Tuna with Summer Nectarine Salsa

Serves 2

A fresh tuna steak has all the dense meatiness of a steak. And with this fruity citrus salsa, it is both elegant and festive. You can make the salsa a couple of days ahead, or just before you put the tuna steaks on the grill.

2 (6-ounce) 1-inch-thick tuna steaks
2 teaspoons olive oil
1 tablespoon cracked black pepper

Nectarine Salsa

2 medium plum tomatoes, coarsely chopped
10 to 12 yellow teardrop tomatoes, quartered
½ red onion, minced
½ jalapeño pepper without seeds, minced
½ (15-ounce) can black beans
1 ripe nectarine, peeled and coarsely chopped
Juice of 1 lime
Pinch of cayenne pepper
¼ teaspoon salt
2 scant tablespoons cider vinegar
3 tablespoons olive oil

1. Heat the grill to medium. Rub both sides of the tuna steaks with the olive oil and cover both sides with the cracked black pepper.

2. To make the salsa: In a medium mixing bowl, combine the tomatoes, onion, jalapeño pepper, black beans, and nectarine. Add the remaining ingredients and stir until completely mixed.

3. Place the steaks on the grill and cook for 3 to 4 minutes per side. The steaks should be seared on the outside and a nice deep pink color on the inside. To serve, place the tuna steaks on individual plates and spoon the salsa over the top.

Roasted **Corn Salad** with Avocado Vinaigrette

Serves 2 to 3

This dish is marvelous in the summer with grilled chicken, swordfish, tuna, or steak.

Avocado Vinaigrette

½ *avocado, chopped*
¼ *cup olive oil*
2 *tablespoons white wine vinegar*
1 *tablespoon freshly squeezed lemon juice*
Dash of Tabasco sauce
½ *teaspoon salt*
½ *teaspoon pepper*

4 *ears of corn, shaved*
3 *teaspoons olive oil*
½ *red bell pepper, finely chopped*
¼ *avocado, thinly sliced*
4 *butter lettuce leaves*
1 *tablespoon coarsely chopped fresh tarragon, for garnish*

1. To make the vinaigrette: Puree the ingredients in a blender and pulse until smooth. Set aside.

2. Heat 1½ teaspoons of the oil in a cast-iron pan over medium heat. Sauté the pepper until soft. Place it in a small bowl and set aside.

3. Heat the remaining 1½ teaspoons olive oil in a cast-iron pan over medium heat. Add the corn, spreading it evenly over the bottom of the pan. As the kernels brown, turn with a metal spatula. Cook for 4 minutes. Stir in the red peppers and cook for 1 to 2 minutes.

4. Spoon corn mixture into a medium bowl and toss with vinaigrette. Place a lettuce leaf on each plate and fill with corn salad. Top with sliced avocados, sprinkle with the tarragon, and serve.

Homemade **Yogurt Cheese** with Marinated Cherries

Serves 2

This is an easy, healthy dessert. The yogurt cheese is so simple to prepare that we usually make some extra just to have it around. It's a wonderful substitute for sour cream or cream cheese. We like the cherries steeped in port and then spooned over the yogurt, but any fresh, ripe summer fruit will do.

1 (8-ounce) container of plain whole milk or lowfat yogurt (no gelatin added)

Marinated cherries

1 cup ruby port
¼ cup sugar
1 whole vanilla bean
8 ounces Bing cherries, with stems

1. Line a colander or large sieve with a double layer of damp cheesecloth. Add the yogurt and place over a medium container that will hold the liquid as it drips through the cheesecloth. Place the yogurt and container in the refrigerator for 8 to 24 hours, depending on how thick you want the yogurt cheese. When the cheese has thickened, place in a covered container in the refrigerator.

2. To make the Marinated Cherries: Combine the port, sugar, and vanilla bean in a small, nonreactive saucepan over low heat. Bring the mixture to a simmer, stirring occasionally. Add the cherries. The liquid should cover the cherries completely; add a little water if necessary. Gently simmer the cherries until tender, 7 to 10 minutes.

3. Remove the pan from the heat and let the cherries stand in the liquid until cooled, about 30 minutes.

4. Remove the cherries with a slotted spoon and place in a medium bowl. Return the pan to high heat and simmer until the liquid is reduced by half. Remove and discard the vanilla bean. Set aside and let cool.

5. To serve, place yogurt in individual bowls, spoon cherries over yogurt, and pour sauce over the top.

DINNER FOR 4

Summer Sangria

◆

Savory Goat Cheese Spread with Endive

◆

Fresh California Corn Chowder

◆

*Rustic Herbed Tomato Tart with
a Parmesan Crust*

◆

*Arugula with Slow-Roasted Shallots
and Toasted Pecans*

◆

Aunt Jennie's Mixed Summer Fruit Cobbler

◆

Vanilla Bean Ice Cream

Menu Manager

Up to 3 days before dinner: **1.** Prepare Vanilla Bean Ice Cream

Day of dinner: **1.** Prepare sangria except for fruit, and chill
2. Prepare Savory Goat Cheese Spread with Endive, and chill
3. Prepare Fresh California Corn Chowder
4. Prepare Parmesan crust for Rustic Herbed Tomato Tart, and refrigerate
5. Prepare topping for Aunt Jennie's Mixed Summer Fruit Cobbler, and refrigerate
6. Toast pecans for Arugula with Slow-Roasted Shallots

About 2 hours before serving: **1.** Preheat oven to 425 degrees and prepare Slow-Roasted Shallots

1 hour before friends arrive: **1.** Prepare fruit, add to sangria, and refrigerate

About 1 hour before serving: **1.** Preheat oven to 425 degrees for tart, bring Parmesan crust to room temperature, prepare and bake Rustic Herbed Tomato Tart

Just before serving dinner: **1.** Lower oven temperature to 325 degrees to reheat cobbler for about 10 to 15 minutes before serving
2. Place ice cream in refrigerator to soften

Summer **Sangria**

Serves 4

This is a drink you can serve all summer long. Just vary the fruit depending on what is available. Chill the sangria ahead so it is ready to pour as soon as your friends arrive.

1 bottle dry white wine
2 cups club soda
4 tablespoons Cointreau
2 tablespoons superfine sugar
½ peach, cut into 1-inch cubes
1 small ripe pear, cut into 1-inch cubes
8 to 10 seedless green grapes
4 to 5 strawberries
Mint sprigs, for garnish

1. Combine the wine, club soda, Cointreau, and sugar in a large pitcher and refrigerate for 2 to 3 hours.

2. Add the peach, pear, grapes, and strawberries about 1 hour before serving and return to refrigerator.

3. To serve, pour sangria and fruit into tall glasses filled with ice. Garnish with a mint sprig.

Savory **Goat Cheese Spread** with Endive

Serves 4

The rich, creamy cheese contrasted with the bitter crunch of the endive keeps the gathering content until dinner time.

8 ounces goat cheese or whipped cream cheese

2 cloves garlic, minced

1 tablespoon finely chopped fresh tarragon

1 tablespoon finely chopped fresh oregano

1 tablespoon finely chopped fresh chives

1 tablespoon cracked black pepper

2 tablespoons heavy whipping cream

3 whole endives

1. Put the cheese, garlic, herbs, and pepper in a medium bowl. Thoroughly mix the ingredients, making sure the herbs and garlic are blended throughout the spread. Gradually stir in the cream to loosen the cheese.

2. Pull the leaves off the endive. Using a damp paper towel, wipe the leaves clean. Discard the small bitter center of the leaves.

3. Use the blade of a dull knife to fill the leaves with the cheese spread. Arrange the filled leaves on a decorative plate and serve.

Fresh California **Corn Chowder**

Serves 4

This creamy yet creamless soup is a wonderful combination of the subtle, sweet taste of corn and the spicy, tangy, peppery tastes of jalapeño, lime, and cilantro. If fresh corn is not available, frozen sweet corn is fine to use. The cilantro adds a punch, so feel free to use as much as you desire.

5 ears of corn, or 4 cups corn kernels
2 tablespoons butter
2 medium leeks, white part only, coarsely chopped
1 rib celery, diced
1 small jalapeño, finely minced
3 cups strained vegetable stock or chicken stock
Juice of 2 limes
2 cups milk
Salt and freshly ground black pepper, to taste
½ medium avocado, cut into 16 thin slices, for garnish
6 tablespoons coarsely chopped fresh cilantro, for garnish

1. Cut the kernels off the ears of corn and set them aside.

2. In a stockpot, melt the butter over medium heat. Add the leeks, celery, and jalapeño. Sauté until the leeks are translucent and the celery and jalapeño are soft. Add the corn and stir for 2 to 3 minutes, making sure that it is thoroughly combined. Add the chicken stock and lime juice and cook for 15 minutes.

3. In a food processor or a blender, puree the soup 2 cups at a time.

4. Return the soup to the stockpot and slowly stir in the milk. Cook for 5 minutes, or until completely warm. Season with salt and pepper.

5. Ladle into 4 bowls. Garnish each with 4 avocado slices and 1½ tablespoons cilantro.

Rustic Herbed **Tomato Tart** with a **Parmesan Crust**

Serves 4

This savory entrée takes advantage of the ripe tomatoes and fresh herbs only summer can offer. It's a perfect meatless meal, bursting with flavor. We also serve this tart as a starter. If there are any leftovers, try it for breakfast.

Pastry

1½ cups all-purpose flour
½ cup (1 stick) unsalted cold butter, cut into 5 pieces
½ teaspoon salt
½ cup freshly grated Parmesan cheese
Zest from ½ lemon
¼ cup ice water

Filling

1½ to 2 tablespoons Dijon mustard
2 tablespoons freshly grated Parmesan cheese
2 tablespoons finely chopped fresh basil
1 tablespoon finely chopped fresh thyme
1 tablespoon finely chopped Italian parsley
2 cloves garlic, minced
Salt and freshly ground black pepper, to taste
6 to 8 ripe plum tomatoes (about 1¼ pounds),
        cut into ¼-inch-thick slices
1 tablespoon olive oil
1 egg yolk beaten with 1 teaspoon water

1. To prepare the pastry: In a food processor fitted with the metal blade, combine the flour, butter, salt, and Parmesan cheese. Pulse until mixture resembles coarse meal, about 5 to 10 seconds. With the motor running, add the lemon zest and pour the water through the feeder tube in a steady stream. Process 5 to 10 seconds, until the dough begins to bind. Remove the dough and shape it into a 12-inch disk. If mixing by hand or with a pastry blender, rub the butter with the flour and the salt until it resembles the size of small peas. Add the lemon zest and Parmesan cheese and combine. Slowly add the ice water, stirring with a fork until dough starts holding together. Shape the dough into a disk.

2. The dough can be used immediately or wrapped in plastic and refrigerated. When ready to use, remove dough from refrigerator and let soften to room temperature, about 30 minutes.

3. Preheat the oven to 425 degrees.

4. On a lightly floured surface, roll the dough into a 12-inch circle. Transfer to a baking sheet. Using a pastry brush, paint the pastry with the mustard, leaving a 1- to 1½-inch border all around. Sprinkle the Parmesan cheese evenly over the mustard.

5. In a small bowl, combine the basil, thyme, parsley, garlic, salt, and pepper. Arrange half of the tomato slices over the mustard-coated portion of the pastry, and sprinkle the herb mixture over the tomatoes. Cover the herbs with the remaining tomatoes, overlapping the slices if necessary.

6. Fold the pastry in half over the tomatoes to enclose the sides of the tart, gently draping the pastry over the tomatoes and folding it into soft pleats every few inches. Pinch any cracks to seal the pastry and prevent tomato juices from running out during baking. Drizzle the olive oil over the tomatoes. Using a pastry brush, paint the dough with the egg wash. Place the tart in the oven and bake for 20 to 25 minutes, or until the dough is golden. Remove tart and let cool slightly, about 10 minutes. Slice and serve warm.

Arugula with Slow-Roasted Shallots and Toasted Pecans

Serves 4

The peppery crunch of arugula is delicious with the sweet, caramelized shallots. We serve this as part of a vegetarian meal, but it is also a flavorful accompaniment to fish, fowl, or beef.

8 shallots, peeled and ends trimmed
2 tablespoons olive oil
3 tablespoons balsamic vinegar

Vinaigrette

1 teaspoon Dijon mustard
½ teaspoon freshly squeezed lemon juice
1 teaspoon balsamic vinegar
4 teaspoons olive oil
Salt and freshly ground black pepper, to taste

¼ cup pecan pieces
3 bunches arugula leaves, torn into thirds

1. Preheat the oven to 425 degrees. Put the shallots in a large bowl and toss them with the olive oil and balsamic vinegar. Place the shallots on a baking sheet or in a baking dish and bake for 35 to 40 minutes, or until tender.

2. Meanwhile, place the pecan pieces in a pie tin and toast them in the oven for 5 to 7 minutes, checking frequently to make sure they do not burn.

3. To make the vinaigrette: Combine mustard, lemon juice, and balsamic vinegar in a small bowl. Slowly add the olive oil, whisking continually, until mixed and creamy. Add salt and pepper.

4. When shallots are cooked, put arugula in a large serving bowl and toss with pecans and vinaigrette.

5. To serve, put the greens and nuts onto individual plates. Place 2 roasted shallots on top.

Vanilla Bean **Ice Cream**

Makes 1 quart

There is nothing more divine than homemade ice cream. And there's nothing more satisfying or easier than making your own quart at home. Be sure to try the Cognac or cinnamon variations.

1 whole vanilla bean
1 cup whole milk or half-and-half
5 large egg yolks, slightly beaten
¾ cup sugar
⅛ teaspoon salt
2 cups heavy whipping cream

1. Split the vanilla bean in half lengthwise. Scrape the beans into a medium saucepan and add the vanilla pod and the milk. Bring to a low simmer over low heat. Remove and discard vanilla pod.

2. Meanwhile, in the bottom of a double boiler, bring about 2 inches of water to a simmer. In the top of a double boiler, off the heat, whisk or beat the egg yolks with the sugar and salt until the sugar is dissolved and the mixture is pale yellow. Add ½ cup of the hot milk to the egg mixture and whisk. Slowly add the remaining milk, and continue whisking until combined.

3. Place the double boiler over the simmering water. Make sure the water does not touch the bottom of the pan. Stir constantly until the mixture thickens enough to coat the back of a spoon, about 10 minutes (times vary, so keep checking).

4. Remove custard from the heat and stir in the cream. Strain through a fine sieve into a medium container and cover. Refrigerate mixture for 2 to 3 hours, and then freeze in an ice cream maker according to manufacturer's instructions.

Variations

Cinnamon Ice Cream: Add ½ teaspoon ground cinnamon in Step 2.
Cognac Ice Cream: Add 2 tablespoons Cognac to the mixture just before freezing it in the ice cream maker.

Aunt Jennie's Mixed Summer Fruit Cobbler

Serves 4 to 6

Ellen considers her Aunt Jennie's mixed fruit cobbler the best she's ever eaten. A few adjustments have been made over the years, and now you too can enjoy this Rose family summer treat. It's terrific served with homemade vanilla ice cream.

¼ cup walnuts, finely chopped

Topping

½ cup (1 stick) unsalted butter, at room temperature
¼ cup confectioners' sugar
Pinch of salt
¼ teaspoon vanilla extract
1 cup all-purpose flour

Filling

5 cups mixed fresh fruit, such as peeled, sliced peaches or nectarines,
*   and blueberries or blackberries*
½ cup granulated sugar (or more, depending on sweetness of fruit)
2 tablespoons all-purpose flour
Pinch of salt
Vanilla Bean Ice Cream (page 55)

1. Preheat the oven to 325 degrees. Butter the bottom and sides of an 8- or 9-inch square baking pan. Put the chopped walnuts in the pan and toast in the oven for 6 to 8 minutes.

2. To prepare topping: In the bowl of an electric mixer, combine butter and confectioners' sugar and beat until fluffy, 1 to 2 minutes. Add the salt and vanilla and beat for another minute. Add the flour and beat until just combined. Stir in the nuts by hand. Roll the dough between two sheets of waxed paper into a square the size of the baking pan. Refrigerate until ready to use.

3. To prepare the filling: Place the fruit, sugar, flour, and salt in a large mixing bowl and stir to combine. Spread the mixture evenly in the prepared pan.

4. Bake in the oven for 10 minutes, or until the filling is hot and bubbling. Remove the pan from the oven.

5. Remove the dough from the refrigerator. Peel off the top layer of waxed paper, place the dough on the fruit, and peel off the remaining piece of waxed paper. Tuck any overhanging pieces of dough between the fruit and the sides of the pan. Cut 3 or 4 small decorative slits in the dough with the tip of a sharp knife. Return the pan to the oven and bake for 20 to 25 minutes, or until the crust is pale golden.

6. While the cobbler is still warm, run the blade of a small knife around the edges of the pan to loosen. Serve warm with a scoop of Vanilla Bean Ice Cream.

6

*Vodka Pink Lemonade with Mint
and Lemon Slices*

♦

Grilled Shrimp with Garlic Aioli

♦

Our Favorite Tuscan Grilled Chicken

♦

Country Mixed Rice Salad

♦

Grilled Seasonal Vegetables

♦

*Grilled Peaches with a Chunk of Bittersweet
Chocolate and Vanilla Bean Ice Cream*

Menu Manager

Up to 3 days before dinner: **1.** Prepare Vanilla Bean Ice Cream

1 night before dinner: **1.** Marinate chicken overnight in refrigerator, turning several times
2. Prepare Garlic Aioli

Day of dinner: **1.** Prepare Vodka Pink Lemonade, but do not add vodka
2. Prepare Country Mixed Rice Salad and let it come to room temperature before adding dressing
3. Prepare the vegetables to be grilled and set aside

When friends arrive: **1.** Add vodka to pink lemonade mixture and serve

1 hour before serving: **1.** Heat the grill or preheat oven if roasting the chicken
2. Bring chicken to room temperature
3. Grill shrimp
4. Prepare and cook chicken
5. Grill vegetables
6. Remove Vanilla Bean Ice Cream from freezer and place in refrigerator to soften

After dinner, while coals are still hot: **1.** Prepare grilled peaches with chocolate and serve immediately with Homemade Vanilla Ice Cream

Vodka **Pink Lemonade** with Mint and Lemon Slices

Serves 6

This drink couldn't be more delicious on a hot summer night. Just watch out—they go down easily! The lemonade is best made the night before, so that the mint has time to impart its flavors.

1 (12-ounce) can pink lemonade concentrate
4 cups water (or follow instructions on can)
2 to 3 lemons, sliced in disks
25 sprigs of mint
9 ounces vodka

1. Defrost the lemonade concentrate for 30 minutes before using. Put the concentrate into a large pitcher and add the water. Stir thoroughly. Add the lemon and mint. Refrigerate for at least 1 hour before serving.

2. Place several ice cubes in a 12- or 14-ounce glass. Add 1½ ounces vodka to each glass and pour the lemonade to fill the glass. Using a fork, take a sprig of mint and a disk of lemon from the pitcher, place them in the glass, and serve.

Grilled Shrimp with Garlic Aioli

Serves 6

This starter is not only delicious, it's a bit of messy fun and it's perfect for a group, with everyone peeling and dipping together. The smoky, salty taste of the shrimp mixed with the creamy garlic aioli is absolutely delicious.

30 medium or large shrimp
2 tablespoons olive oil
2 cloves garlic, minced

Garlic Aioli

3 medium cloves garlic, mashed and then chopped
2 egg yolks
¾ cup olive oil
1 tablespoon freshly squeezed lemon juice

1. Heat the grill.

2. Wash the shrimp with shells on and pat dry with a paper towel.

3. Put the olive oil and garlic in a bowl and stir to combine. Take a skewer and prick the shrimp in the center of its body. Follow with the other shrimp, making sure they are evenly placed and not crammed together. Brush the shrimp on both sides with the olive oil-garlic mixture.

4. To make the Garlic Aioli: Combine the 3 cloves of garlic with the egg yolks in a small bowl. Pour the mixture into a blender or the bowl of a food processor fitted with the metal blade. Gradually add the olive oil in a steady stream with the machine running. Stop mixing, add the lemon juice, and blend the ingredients for another 30 seconds. Spoon the sauce into a small serving bowl.

5. Place the skewers on the hot grill and cook for 2 to 3 minutes on each side. As the shrimp cooks, lightly brush the meat with the garlic-olive oil mixture. Immediately remove the shrimp from the skewers. Arrange shrimp on a platter in an attractive presentation around the aioli, and serve.

Our Favorite Tuscan **Grilled Chicken**

Serves 6

We love this rustic way of preparing chicken. You can cook the chicken on the grill in the warm weather, or roast it in a hot oven in the colder months.

Marinade

½ cup olive oil
Juice of 2 lemons or limes
3 cloves garlic, flattened
⅛ cup chopped fresh rosemary
¼ cup chopped fresh Italian parsley
Salt and freshly ground black pepper, to taste

2 (3- to 4-pound) chickens, butterflied and backbone removed
2 to 3 quartered or sliced lemons or limes, for garnish
5 to 6 sprigs of rosemary, for garnish

1. To grill or roast, combine all of the ingredients for marinade in a medium bowl. Place the chicken in a large bowl, pour marinade over chicken, and cover and refrigerate overnight, turning occasionally.

2. To grill chicken, heat the grill to medium-hot. Remove the chicken from the marinade and pat dry. Reserve the marinade. Put chicken on the grill skin side down and place a heavy weight on top of chicken—a cast-iron skillet or a brick wrapped in aluminum foil works well. Cook for 10 to 12 minutes, basting with reserved marinade. Turn chicken and grill an additional 15 minutes.

3. To roast chicken, preheat the oven to 425 degrees. Remove the chicken from the marinade and pat dry. Reserve the marinade. Heat one or two cast-iron or other heavy pans until very hot. Place chicken in the heated pans skin side down, and weight chicken with foil-wrapped bricks, heavy cans, or ano-ther heavy pan. Cook for 5 to 7 minutes. Remove the weights and place in the oven for 15 minutes; baste frequently with the reserved marinade. Turn, baste, and cook for about 20 minutes longer. Check for doneness. The juices should run clear. Serve with lemon or lime slices and rosemary.

Country Mixed **Rice Salad**

Serves 6

Serve this salad either at room temperature or chilled. Try using a colorful variety of tomatoes for a little added flavor.

3 cups water
½ teaspoon salt
¾ cup wild rice, rinsed
½ cup long-grain white rice
½ cup toasted pecans
6 cherry tomatoes, quartered
6 yellow teardrop tomatoes, quartered
½ cup kalamata olives, pitted and quartered

2 tablespoons finely chopped fresh thyme
¼ cup chopped fresh basil

Dressing
3 tablespoons white wine vinegar
1 tablespoon freshly squeezed lemon juice
1 teaspoon Dijon mustard
⅓ cup olive oil
Salt and freshly ground black pepper, to taste

1. Place 2 cups of the water and ¼ teaspoon of the salt in a medium saucepan over medium heat. Stir in the wild rice and bring to a boil. Reduce the heat to low, cover tightly, and simmer until the rice is tender, 40 to 50 minutes. Put rice in a serving bowl and let cool.

2. Combine the remaining 1 cup of water with the remaining ¼ teaspoon salt in a small saucepan over medium heat. Bring to a boil. Add the white rice, reduce the heat to low, cover tightly, and simmer until the rice is tender, about 20 minutes. Transfer to the serving bowl with the wild rice and stir to combine.

3. To toast the pecans: Preheat the oven to 325 degrees. Put the pecans in a single layer on a baking sheet. Toast for 5 to 8 minutes, remove from the oven, and let cool.

4. Add the toasted pecans, cherry tomatoes, yellow tomatoes, olives, thyme, and basil to the rice and toss gently to combine.

5. To make the dressing: In a small bowl, whisk together the vinegar, lemon juice, and mustard. Slowly whisk in the olive oil until it is incorporated. Season with salt and pepper, whisking to combine. Pour over the salad and toss well.

Grilled Seasonal **Vegetables**

Serves 6

When vegetables are grilled they acquire an unbeatable smoky sweetness. Feel free to experiment with your favorite vegetables. Just keep in mind that the thickness of the vegetable is important if you do not have a small-grid grill. You may want to place a second grid on top of your regular grill; two grids form a sort of mesh, preventing the vegetables from dropping into the fire. Metal grids of various sizes are available at hardware and home supply stores.

12 to 14 scallions
2 red bell peppers, seeded, deribbed, and cut into 1½-inch vertical slices
2 to 3 radicchio leaves, cut into ½-inch vertical slices
2 zucchini, cut into ½-inch vertical slices
6 tablespoons olive oil
Salt and freshly ground black pepper, to taste
2 tablespoons balsamic vinegar
Juice of ½ lemon
6 sprigs of rosemary, for garnish

1. Heat the grill to medium.

2. Rub all of the vegetables lightly with the olive oil and season with salt and pepper. Reserve some of the olive oil for drizzling.

3. Grill until golden brown, 6 to 12 minutes, turning as the vegetables brown.

4. When the vegetables are cooked, drizzle them with the remaining olive oil and the vinegar. Place on a serving platter. Sprinkle with lemon juice and garnish with rosemary.

Grilled Peaches with a Chunk of Bittersweet Chocolate and Vanilla Bean Ice Cream

Serves 6

The taste of fresh summer peaches and warm bittersweet chocolate combine to make one of our favorite summer desserts. The cool ice cream counterbalances the warmth of the peach and chocolate. Homemade ice cream is a real treat, but you can use store-bought vanilla ice cream if you don't have the time or equipment to make it at home. A gas grill makes this a bit easier, but a charcoal grill will work just as well. Just throw a few extra briquettes on the fire after you finish cooking the Tuscan chicken, and the grill should be ready later on for dessert. These peaches can also be prepared in the oven.

2 tablespoons butter, melted
6 large ripe peaches, halved and pitted
6½ ounces bittersweet chocolate, broken into ½-ounce pieces
Vanilla Bean Ice Cream (page 55)

1. Wipe off the grill to make a clean surface. When the grill is medium hot place the peaches directly on the grill, flesh side down. Cook for 3 to 5 minutes, or until peaches begin to brown slightly. Remove peaches and cover the grill surface with a large piece of aluminum foil.

2. Return peaches to the grill, flesh side up. Place a ½-ounce chunk of chocolate in the well of each peach half. Using a pastry brush, coat the peaches with the melted butter. Cover the grill and cook for 20 to 25 minutes, or until the peaches are soft and tender all the way through.

3. To prepare in the oven: Preheat the oven to 425 degrees. Follow the directions in Step 3 for preparing peaches with chocolate and melted butter, and on a baking sheet roast the peaches for 15 to 20 minutes.

4. To serve, place 2 peach halves in a shallow bowl and serve with a scoop of Vanilla Bean Ice Cream.

F ◆ A

In fall, the days shorten, temperatures drop, and the landscape of summer's brilliant green turns to gold, orange, and rusty red. We come inside for our first cozy fire. We invite a couple or two over for a simple, warm meal. Pure comfort food.

The fall finds us moving away from the light fare of summer and turning to heartier savory foods. A juicy Pork Tenderloin with Fall Fruits in a Reduced Port Sauce served with Perfect Mashed Potatoes warms our tummies. More substantial main dishes like Wide Noodles with Mussel in Mustard Cream and Fennel, Mascarpone, and Fresh Herb Risotto are perfect in the fall. Fall fruits and vegetables such as pears, apples, figs, mushrooms, and rapini appear at the markets in abundance. You'll find the best of the season's harvest in our menus—from Crostini with Two Toppings, to Rapini with Garlic and Olive Oil, to Roasted Fall Figs with a Brown Sugar Crust and Crème Fraîche. Our Autumn Mixed Nut Tart is so delicious that friends devour it within minutes and beg for more.

L · L

DINNER FOR

2

Hot and Spicy Flavored Nuts

•

*Pork Tenderloin with Fall Fruits in a
Reduced Port Sauce*

•

Rapini with Garlic and Olive Oil

•

Perfect Mashed Potatoes

•

*Sautéed Caramelized Apple Slices with
Cinnamon Ice Cream*

Menu Manager

Up to 1 month before dinner: **1.** Prepare Hot and Spicy Flavored Nuts and store in the refrigerator in an airtight container

2 to 3 days ahead: **1.** Prepare Cinnamon Ice Cream

About 1 hour before serving: **1.** Prepare Fall Fruits in a Reduced Port Sauce
2. Prepare Perfect Mashed Potatoes
3. Prepare Pork Tenderloin
4. Prepare Rapini with Garlic and Olive Oil
5. Slice apples for Sautéed Camelized Apple Slices and place in lemon water.

After dinner: **1.** Remove ice cream from freezer to soften
2. Prepare Sautéed Caramelized Apple Slices and serve over ice cream

Hot and Spicy **Flavored Nuts**

Makes 2 cups

We have learned that it's a good idea to keep some flavored nuts and marinated olives on hand. Both will keep for months refrigerated in an airtight container. These buttery toasted nuts flavored with cumin, cayenne, and cinnamon make a delightful, savory before-dinner snack.

1 tablespoon unsalted butter

1 teaspoon ground cumin

1 teaspoon cayenne pepper

1 teaspoon ground cinnamon

½ cup whole cashews

½ cup blanched whole almonds

½ cup peeled hazelnuts

½ cup pecan halves

1 teaspoon salt

1. Melt the butter in a medium saucepan. Add the spices and sauté for 2 to 3 minutes over low heat, or until the spices become fragrant. Add the nuts, stirring until they are coated with spicy butter mixture. Continue sautéing until the nuts are toasted, 8 to 10 minutes. Remove from the heat and let cool completely before serving.

Rapini with Garlic and Olive Oil

Serves 2

This bitter green is an Italian favorite. It looks like a baby broccoli, but it is actually a member of the turnip family. Rapini may be an acquired taste, but once you've had it a couple of times, it becomes an addiction.

2 bunches of rapini
¼ cup water
½ teaspoon salt
2½ tablespoons olive oil
2 cloves garlic, thinly sliced
½ teaspoon anchovy paste
¼ teaspoon crushed red pepper flakes
Juice of ½ lemon
¼ cup freshly grated Parmesan cheese

1. Cut the rapini into thirds, discarding the bottom inch of the stem. Place the water and salt in a large stockpot and bring to a boil over medium-high heat. When it reaches a rapid boil, reduce heat to medium and add the rapini. Cook for 8 minutes, or until tender.

2. Meanwhile, in a large saucepan, heat the olive oil over medium heat. Add the garlic and sauté for 1 minute, making sure it doesn't brown. Turn off the heat.

3. Transfer the rapini to a colander to drain. Press the rapini against the side of the colander with a large spoon or spatula to remove all excess water.

4. Add the rapini to the saucepan with the garlic and sauté for about 2 minutes. Add the anchovy paste, crushed red pepper flakes, and lemon juice. Stir the rapini for 1 minute more.

5. Place rapini in a serving bowl, sprinkle with Parmesan, and serve.

Pork Tenderloin with Fall Fruits in a Reduced Port Sauce

Serves 2

A pork tenderloin is the perfect size for two people. It is both quick and festive, and it's one of our favorite comfort foods on a chilly, crisp evening. The tender pork with the sweet dried fruit macerated in port is simply delicious. We like dried apricots and pitted prunes with this, but a combination of these and dried pears and peaches adds a nice variety. This is a dinner to linger over with someone special.

1 tablespoon unsalted butter
1 (8-ounce) package mixed dried fruit,
*   or a selection of your favorite dried fruit*
½ cup freshly squeezed orange juice
¼ cup port
1 pork tenderloin (about 1½ pounds)
1 tablespoon olive oil
1 tablespoon unsalted butter
Salt and freshly ground black pepper, to taste

Sauce

½ cup port
1½ to 2 cups beef or chicken stock

1. Preheat the oven to 450 degrees.

2. Heat the butter in a small, heavy saucepan. Add dried fruit, orange juice, and port. Cook over medium-low heat for 5 to 10 minutes, until fruit is soft and liquid has thickened. Set aside.

3. Heat the oil and butter in a sauté pan or heavy casserole large enough to hold the pork tenderloin. Pat pork dry with paper towels. Season with salt and pepper. Brown pork well on all sides over medium heat for 8 to 10 minutes.

4. Add the macerated fruit with the liquid to pan. Add the beef or chicken broth. Cover and cook over medium heat until pork is tender, about 10 to 15 minutes. The temperature should reach 150 degrees on an instant-read meat thermometer. Remove pork and fruit from the oven and let rest about 10 minutes before carving.

5. To make the sauce: Add the port to the pan and scrape up all the brown bits from the sides and bottom of the pan. Bring to a simmer and reduce the sauce, simmering uncovered until thickened. If more sauce is desired, add another cup or so of stock and simmer and reduce again.

6. Slice pork into ½- to ¾-inch slices and place on a serving platter. Arrange fruit around pork and drizzle with sauce. Serve immediately.

🌺 Perfect Mashed **Potatoes**

Serves 2

This easy recipe proves that less is more—these mashed potatoes are as delicious as the sinful mashed potatoes of the past but are not even a quarter as fattening. If Yukon Gold potatoes are not available, substitute new potatoes.

3 to 4 medium to large Yukon Gold potatoes, peeled and coarsely chopped
Pinch of salt
¾ cup warm milk, or as needed
Freshly ground white pepper, to taste

1. Put potatoes and salt in a medium saucepan with water to cover and bring to a boil. Lower heat and simmer until the potatoes are tender, 10 to 15 minutes. Check potatoes frequently and do not overcook.

2. Drain potatoes and mash in a ricer, a food mill, or with a handheld potato masher.

3. Add the warm milk gradually until the desired consistency is reached. Stir in pepper. Serve the potatoes in a small terrine or serving dish.

Sautéed Caramelized **Apple Slices** with Cinnamon Ice Cream

Serves 2

We serve this warm, gooey dessert with homemade Cinnamon Ice Cream, a variation of our Vanilla Bean Ice Cream, or a good quality ice cream can be bought. This simple dessert is perfect enjoyed on a cool fall night in front of the fire or at the table in a warm kitchen.

1 apple, peeled, cored, and cut in half
½ lemon

3 tablespoons butter
1 tablespoon sugar
¼ teaspoon ground cinnamon

Cinnamon Ice Cream (page 55)

1. Cut each apple half into 6 slices. Squeeze the lemon juice into a medium bowl of cold water, deep enough to cover the apples. Place the apples slices in the lemon water.

2. Combine the butter and sugar in a medium skillet over medium heat. As the butter melts, swirl the pan to combine the butter with the sugar. Remove the apple slices from the water and pat them dry with paper towels. Add the apples to the pan, lower the heat, and shake the pan to evenly disperse the apples. Cook, turning the apple slices frequently until they are golden, about 5 to 7 minutes. Sprinkle the apples with the cinnamon, cook for 1 minute more, and remove from the heat.

3. Serve immediately in individual bowls over a scoop of Cinnamon Ice Cream.

DINNER FOR

Crostini with Two Toppings

◆

Fennel, Mascarpone, and Fresh Herb Risotto

◆

Mixed Green Salad with
Elizabeth's Parmesan Wafers

◆

Autumn Mixed Nut Tart

Menu Manager

Up to 5 days before dinner: **1.** Prepare Elizabeth's Parmesan Wafers and store in an airtight container

1 day before or day of dinner: **1.** Prepare Autumn Mixed Nut Tart

Day of dinner: **1.** Prepare crostini toppings
2. Prepare salad dressing and wash and crisp greens

30 minutes before serving: **1.** Prepare toasts for crostini
2. Prepare Fennel, Mascarpone, and Fresh Herb Risotto

Crostini with Two Toppings: Wild Mushroom and Fried Rosemary and Broiled Eggplant with Basil Garlic Cream

Serves 4

Crostini, which means "little toasts" in Italian, are typically served as appetizers or snacks. These two toppings are made from the meatiest of vegetables, giving substance to this vegetarian menu. The toppings can be made up to 4 hours ahead.

1 large baguette, cut into ½-inch slices on the diagonal

Wild Mushroom Topping

3 tablespoons olive oil
4 shallots, coarsely chopped
8 shiitake mushrooms, minced
8 button mushrooms, minced
10 oyster mushrooms, minced
1 medium portobello mushroom, minced
¼ cup sherry
Salt and freshly ground black pepper, to taste
4 sprigs of rosemary

Broiled Eggplant Topping

4 Japanese eggplant, sliced ¼-inch-thick lengthwise
Salt
4 tablespoons pine nuts
½ cup chopped fresh basil
4 cloves garlic, minced
½ cup freshly grated Parmesan cheese
½ tablespoon balsamic vinegar
3 tablespoons olive oil

1. To make the Wild Mushroom Topping: In a large saucepan over medium heat, add 2 tablespoons of the olive oil to coat the bottom of the pan. Heat oil for 1 minute. Add the shallots and sauté until soft. Add the mushrooms, stirring until they are covered with the oil and shallots. When the mushrooms begin to release their juices, pour in the sherry. Simmer for 10 to 12 minutes, stirring occasionally. Add salt and freshly ground black pepper, to taste. When the mushrooms are cooked, turn off heat and keep in pan. Meanwhile, in a small frying pan heat the remaining olive oil for 2 to 3 minutes, or until it begins to bubble. Place the rosemary sprigs into the oil and let them sizzle for 3 minutes. Remove the rosemary and place it on several thicknesses of paper towels to drain. Set aside.

2. To make the Broiled Eggplant Topping: Preheat the broiler. Place the eggplant slices on a plate and lightly salt them, layering them one slice on top of the other. Let sit for 15 minutes. Meanwhile, put the pine nuts in a pie tin and place the pan under the broiler for 1 to 2 minutes. Check the nuts frequently, shaking the pan to ensure even browning. They should be golden brown all over. Pat the eggplant slices dry and place them on the broiler. Cook in the broiler for 2 to 3 minutes per side, turning them when they brown. In a food processor or a blender, combine ¼ cup of the basil, the garlic, Parmesan cheese, vinegar, olive oil, and pine nuts. Pulse the mixture until creamy. Set aside.

3. Put the slices of baguette on a baking sheet and drizzle them with olive oil. Toast slices under the broiler for 1 to 2 minutes, or until golden brown. Turn the slices, drizzle with olive oil, and broil until golden. Remove toasted bread from the broiler. For the crostini with wild mushroom topping, spread each slice evenly with the mushroom topping and place a piece of fried rosemary on top. For the crostini with eggplant topping, spread the toast with the basil mixture, place a piece of eggplant on top, and garnish with a pinch of fresh basil. Arrange the crostini on a large platter and serve.

Crostini

Fennel, Mascarpone, and Fresh Herb Risotto

Serves 4

Risotto is a perfect comfort food for a small dinner party. We invite our guests into the kitchen for conversation while we stir. This risotto combines the refreshing licorice taste of fennel with the rich, buttery flavor of mascarpone cheese.

2 tablespoons butter
1 tablespoon olive oil
2 cloves garlic, thinly sliced
½ onion, finely chopped
1 fennel bulb, sliced into thin rounds
1½ cups Arborio rice
4 cups strained vegetable stock or chicken stock
1½ cups dry white wine
¼ cup mascarpone cheese (or sour cream)
¼ cup freshly grated Parmesan cheese, plus more for garnish
1 teaspoon minced fresh thyme
1 teaspoon minced fresh marjoram
1 teaspoon minced fresh Italian parsley
Freshly ground black pepper, to taste

1. In a large saucepan, heat the butter and olive oil over medium heat. Add the garlic and onion and sauté for 2 to 3 minutes, or until translucent. Add the fennel and sauté for another 2 to 3 minutes.

2. Add the rice to the pan, and then add some of the wine, waiting until the liquid is nearly absorbed before adding more. Add some of the broth and more of the wine, alternating between the two and waiting until liquid is absorbed before adding more. When all the liquid has been added, cook for about 15 minutes. Add the mascarpone, Parmesan, and herbs to the rice mixture and stir vigorously for 2 to 3 minutes. The rice is ready when it is firm but tender.

3. To serve, spoon the rice into individual serving bowls, and top with Parmesan cheese and freshly ground black pepper.

Mixed **Green Salad** with **Elizabeth's Parmesan Wafers**

Serves 4

Our friend Elizabeth Burns, a woman of great style and grace, serves these wonderful wafers. Easy to make, they can be prepared days ahead and stored in an airtight container.

Parmesan Wafers

2 teaspoons all-purpose flour
1 cup finely grated Parmesan cheese
1 tablespoon unsalted butter, at room temperature

Dressing

2 tablespoons raspberry balsamic vinegar
6 tablespoons extra-virgin olive oil
1 heaping teaspoon Dijon mustard
Salt and freshly ground black pepper, to taste

About 8 cups mixed baby salad greens
¼ cup chopped fresh herbs, such as thyme, basil, marjoram, and mint

1. To make the Parmesan Wafers: Preheat the oven to 350 degrees. Mix flour and Parmesan in a small bowl. Cover a baking sheet with parchment paper. Drop 1 tablespoon of the mixture on the parchment and spread into a 3-inch oval using a spoon. Repeat, spacing at 2-inch intervals.

2. Bake for 8 to 10 minutes, until wafers are lightly golden. They burn quickly, so start checking after 5 minutes. Remove from oven and transfer wafers with a metal spatula to a cooling rack.

3. To make the dressing: In a small bowl, whisk together all ingredients until well blended.

4. Put the greens and herbs in a large salad bowl. Add the dressing and toss lightly. Serve wafers whole either in or beside the salad, or pass separately. Guests can decide whether to crumble the wafers on top or munch on them between bites of salad.

Autumn Mixed **Nut Tart**

Makes 4 generous servings

This dessert was inspired by a nut tart that Nancy Silverton makes to sell at her La Brea Bakery in Los Angeles. But it is only available on weekends and we wanted to be able to enjoy it anytime. Here is our version of this scrumptious dessert. Let it cool for a couple of hours before serving to give it a chance to set.

Pastry

1 cup all-purpose flour
3 tablespoons sugar
¼ teaspoon salt
6 tablespoons unsalted cold butter, cut into 6 pieces
1 large egg, beaten

Filling

¼ cup sugar
¼ cup light corn syrup
2 tablespoons unsalted butter, melted
¾ cup almonds
½ cup cashews
½ cup sliced blanched almonds
¼ cup pepitas (pumpkin seeds)

1. To prepare the pastry: In a food processor fitted with the metal blade, combine the flour, sugar, salt, and butter. Pulse until the mixture resembles coarse crumbs, about 5 to 10 seconds. With the motor running, add the egg through the feeder tube. Process 5 to 10 seconds, until dough begins to pull together. Remove dough, form into a disk, cover in plastic wrap, and refrigerate for 30 minutes. To prepare the pastry by hand, combine the ingredients in a large bowl in the same order. Work the flour and butter together quickly with your fingertips until it resembles coarse crumbs, then add the egg, and blend into the pastry. When dough coheres, form a 5-inch disk, wrap, and refrigerate.

2. Preheat the oven to 375 degrees. Remove dough from refrigerator. With lightly floured hands, pat the chilled pastry into a 7- or 8-inch fluted tart pan with a removable bottom. Cover the tart shell with parchment paper or aluminum foil and fill with pie weights or dried beans. Bake for 10 minutes. Remove paper and weights and return the tart shell to the oven. Bake for 5 minutes more, until the shell is dry but not golden. Remove tart shell from the oven and set aside. Do not turn off oven.

3. To prepare the filling: In a small bowl, combine the sugar, corn syrup, and butter, and stir to combine. Arrange all of the nuts and seeds evenly over the bottom of the tart shell. Pour the sugar mixture over the nuts.

4. Bake tart on the center rack of the oven for 25 to 30 minutes, or until crust and nuts are golden and the edge of the filling is firm. Transfer tart to a wire rack to cool completely, at least 1 hour.

5. Remove rim and place tart on a serving plate. The tart is best served at room temperature.

DINNER FOR

6

Cured Salmon with Thinly Sliced Fennel

♦

*Wide Noodles with Mussels in Mustard Cream
with Leeks, Peas, and Tarragon*

♦

*Baby Spinach with French Feta, Walnuts, and
Roasted Red Bell Peppers*

♦

*Roasted Fall Figs with Brown Sugar Crust and
Crème Fraîche*

Menu Manager

Up to one week before dinner: **1.** Prepare Crème Fraîche and refrigerate

Day of dinner: **1.** Prepare roasted red bell peppers and dressing for salad.

About 1 hour before dinner: **1.** Slice figs
2. Broil figs for 2 to 3 minutes

About 45 minutes before dinner: **1.** Prepared Cured Salmon with Thinly Sliced Fennel
2. Prepare mussels
3. Prepare wide noodles and finish dish
4. Toss spinach salad

When dinner is served: **1.** Preheat broiler for figs again

After dinner: **1.** Cook the syrup for the figs
2. Rebroil figs with syrup
3. Serve roasted figs with crème fraîche

❧ **Cured Salmon** With Thinly Sliced Fennel

Serves 6

We serve this when we want a first course that looks elegant but couldn't be easier to make. The licorice taste of the fennel paired with the delicate cured taste of the salmon is unique, light and clean. It's best to use a smoked Scottish or Irish salmon. Gravlax also works nicely, but it is a bit sweeter than the smoked salmon.

2 medium fennel bulbs
1½ pounds thinly sliced smoked salmon
4 tablespoons capers, drained
3 tablespoons snipped fresh chives
Juice of 4 lemons
Olive oil for drizzling
Salt and cracked black pepper, to taste

1. To prepare fennel, pull the outer leaf off the bulb. Wash the bulb and cut off the very bottom. Thinly slice the bulb into paper-thin slivers. Cut out and discard the round heart in the center of the slivers. You should be left with half-moons of fennel.

2. Arrange the fennel and salmon, alternating the two on individual plates. Sprinkle the capers and chives over the salmon and fennel, squeeze the lemon juice over the top, and drizzle with olive oil. Season with salt and cracked pepper, and serve.

Wide Noodles with Mussels in Mustard Cream with Leeks, Peas, and Tarragon

Serves 6

The aniselike flavor of tarragon adds a tang to the salty-sweet flavors of the mussels and leeks. This dish is rich enough not to beg for Parmesan cheese. All you need is a crisp Pinot Grigio and a good, crusty Italian bread.

2¾ cups dry white wine
2½ pounds black-lipped mussels, scrubbed and debearded
4 tablespoons vegetable oil
1½ tablespoons salt
3 tablespoons Dijon mustard
1 cup heavy whipping cream
3 tablespoons butter
3 tablespoons olive oil
8 large leeks, thinly sliced
2 teaspoons black pepper
2 pounds pappardelle or fettuccini
½ cup fresh tarragon, coarsely chopped
1½ cups fresh or frozen peas

1. Pour 1 cup of the wine in a medium stockpot and heat over medium-high heat. Cover and cook until the wine begins to boil. Add the mussels and cook until they all have opened, about 5 to 7 minutes. Discard any mussels that have not opened. Remove the mussels from their shells and set them aside. Strain the mussel broth over layered cheesecloth into a bowl and reserve.

2. Place 4 quarts of water in a large stockpot. Add the vegetable oil and 1 tablespoon of the salt and bring to a boil.

3. Meanwhile, place the mustard and cream in a small bowl and stir until fully combined. In a large saucepan over low heat, add the butter and olive oil. Stir until the butter has melted. Add the leeks and sauté until translucent.

4. Add the pasta to the boiling water. Check the directions on the box, but usually wide noodles take 7 to 10 minutes.

5. When the leeks are translucent, add the reserved mussel broth and stir until it begins to simmer. Add the mustard cream and the remaining wine. Cook, stirring continually for 5 to 7 minutes to reduce the sauce. The sauce should thicken as it lightly bubbles.

6. When the pasta is almost done (it should be slightly hard in the center), add the tarragon, peas, mussels, ½ tablespoon of the salt, and the pepper to the sauce. Continue cooking the sauce over low heat until the pasta is completely cooked. Drain the pasta in a colander, add it to the sauce, and toss until the sauce fully coats the pasta. Serve immediately.

Baby Spinach with French Feta, Walnuts, and Roasted Red Bell Peppers

Serves 6

Baby spinach is preferable in this dish because it is so sweet and tender, but if it's not available, you can substitute mature spinach. (Just remove the coarse stems and chop the leaves in half.) We also prefer to use French feta because it is creamier and a little less salty than Greek feta. If you do not have the time to roast your own bell peppers, look for bottled roasted peppers in supermarkets and specialty food stores.

1 large red bell pepper
¼ cup chopped walnuts

Vinaigrette

1 clove garlic, minced
2 teaspoons Dijon mustard
2 tablespoons white wine vinegar
Large pinch of sugar
⅛ teaspoon salt
¼ teaspoon black pepper
6 tablespoons olive oil

3 bunches baby spinach, or 2 bunches regular spinach
½ cup crumbled French feta

1. To roast the red bell peppers: Turn the gas burner up to high and hold the pepper close to the flame with a fork. Spin the pepper as it begins to blister. If you don't have a gas burner, roast the pepper under the broiler, turning it as it blisters. Remove the pepper from the heat when it is blistered all over, put it in a plastic bag, and seal it tightly. Let the pepper sweat for 5 minutes, then remove it from the bag and peel it, using your fingers. Cut the pepper lengthwise, remove the seeds, and cut it in ¼-inch-thick slices. Set aside.

2. Preheat the broiler for 2 to 3 minutes. Put the walnuts in a pie pan and toast under the broiler for 3 minutes. Check the walnuts, shaking the pan periodically to toast evenly.

3. To make the vinaigrette: In a medium bowl, place the garlic, Dijon mustard, vinegar, sugar, salt, and pepper. Whisk together into a paste, and then slowly add the olive oil. Whisk until fully combined.

4. Place the spinach in a salad bowl. Add the roasted peppers, feta cheese, and toasted walnuts. Whisk the dressing one last time and add it to the salad. Toss the salad and serve.

Roasted **Fall Figs** with Brown Sugar Crust and Crème Fraîche

Serves 6

This decadent dessert is a wonderful ending to any meal. Serve with ginger-snaps or shortbread. You'll need to make the crème fraîche at least 8 to 12 hours ahead of time; when refrigerated, it will keep for up to 1 week.

Crème Fraîche

1 cup heavy whipping cream
1 teaspoon buttermilk

9 fresh black Mission figs
3 tablespoons butter
6 tablespoons dark brown sugar dissolved in 3 teaspoons water
6 sprigs of mint

1. To make the Crème Fraîche: Over a low flame, heat the cream and buttermilk in a medium saucepan until lukewarm. Put the mixture in a jar or container with a loosely fitting top. Let the mixture sit out at room temperature for 8 to 12 hours.

2. Preheat the broiler. Slice the figs lengthwise. Place them on a baking sheet or pie tin skin side up. Broil for 2 to 3 minutes. Remove the pan from the oven and set aside.

3. Melt the butter and brown sugar mixture in a small saucepan over low heat. Add the water and cook the mixture until it becomes syrupy, about 5 minutes. Stir the mixture occasionally as it cooks.

4. Turn the figs over on the baking sheet and place them under the broiler for 2 minutes, or until the figs brown on the edges. Remove the figs from the broiler and spoon the syrup over them, making sure the syrup only goes on the figs. Place the figs under the broiler for another 2 to 3 minutes, until the syrup begins to bubble and brown.

5. Remove the figs from the broiler. Divide them onto 6 plates and top with a dollop of crème fraîche. Garnish with a sprig of mint and serve.

W·I·N

Winter is the coziest time of year. By winter you've established your place next to the fire, or in that easy chair, or in bed with a warm cup of tea and a book. You're ready to settle in for the duration.

In winter we move indoors, nest, and enjoy the company of family and friends in the comfortable, quiet setting of our homes. The barren landscape inspires us to stay close to the kitchen and to fill up on good conversation and, of course, delicious food.

The fresh fruits and vegetables of winter are limited compared to other times of the year. However, there are still plenty of root vegetables and winter greens that make interesting, tasty side dishes. The textures and flavors of winter foods are creamy, earthy, and dense. Bistro Skillet Steak with Reduced Burgundy Sauce and Cheesy Potato Gratin are two hearty cold-season dishes we like to serve our friends when we share an evening of delicious food and lively conversation. And what could be more satisfying on a winter night than Winter Pot Roast with Juniper Berries? Or a bowl of Fennel Soup with Roasted Garlic Croutons? And for dessert? Caramelized Banana Bread Pudding or Fresh Gingery Gingerbread makes a cold winter night something to look forward to.

T · E · R

DINNER FOR

2

Lamb Chops on Garlicky Winter Greens

♦

Endive, Apple, Blue Cheese, and
Hickory Nut Salad

♦

Cheesy Potato Gratin

♦

Stephen's Cherry Biscotti

Menu Manager

Up to 1 month before dinner: **1.** Prepare biscotti

Day of dinner: **1.** Defrost biscotti if frozen
2. Prepare vinaigrette for salad

About 1 hour before serving: **1.** Preheat oven to 375 degrees for the gratin
2. Prepare and bake Cheesy Potato Gratin
3. Bring lamb to room temperature
4. Prepare Endive, Apple, Blue Cheese, and Hickory Nut Salad
5. Prepare Lamb Chops on Garlicky Winter Greens

Lamb Chops on Garlicky Winter Greens

Serves 2

Lamb chops are perfect for a dinner for two. The seasonal winter greens add a clean bite to the rich, sweet taste of the meat. And the garlic makes the dish—and just about anything—even more delicious.

4 1-inch-thick loin lamb chops, at room temperature

2 garlic cloves, thinly sliced, plus 1 clove cut in half

5 tablespoons olive oil

Salt and freshly ground black pepper, to taste

1 head of radicchio, cut in half and sliced

2 bunches watercress, coarse stems removed

2 bunches fresh spinach, leaves sliced in half

¼ teaspoon crushed red pepper flakes

1. Rub the lamb on all its surfaces with the garlic halves. Drizzle the lamb with 1 tablespoon of the olive oil and season with salt and pepper.

2. Heat 2 tablespoons of the olive oil in a large skillet over medium heat. Add the garlic and sauté for 1 minute, making sure that it doesn't turn brown. Add the radicchio, watercress, and spinach and stir for 1 to 2 minutes. Cover the pan for 1 to 2 minutes, or until the greens are wilted. Add the red pepper flakes and turn off the heat.

3. In a nonstick or cast-iron skillet, heat the remaining 2 tablespoons olive oil until very hot. Add the lamb chops and cook for 3 minutes on each side for rare, 4 minutes on each side for medium.

4. Reheat the greens for 1 minute. Season with salt and pepper. Spread the greens on a round or oval serving platter. Place the chops on top of the greens, and serve.

Cheesy **Potato Gratin**

Serves 2

Yukon Gold potatoes are sweet and tender and when combined with the nutty taste of Gruyère and the savory Parmesan they're even more divine. We add sage because it's a rich, potent spice, but you can add other herbs, such as thyme or marjoram, if you like. Just make sure to use good, fresh cheese; it makes all the difference.

½ tablespoon plus 1 teaspoon butter
½ tablespoon olive oil
1 clove garlic, thinly sliced
4½ fresh sage leaves
5 Yukon Gold potatoes (about ¾ to 1 pound), peeled and thinly sliced
¼ cup grated Gruyère cheese
⅓ cup freshly grated Parmesan cheese
½ teaspoon all-purpose flour
½ cup milk
Salt and freshly ground black pepper, to taste

1. Preheat the oven to 375 degrees. Grease a 9-inch round or oval baking pan with 1 teaspoon of the butter.

2. Melt the remaining butter in a medium saucepan. Add the olive oil and the garlic and sage and sauté for 1 to 2 minutes. The garlic should be soft, but not browned.

3. Carefully place a layer of potatoes in the baking pan. Top potatoes with a few slices of garlic and 1½ sage leaves. Sprinkle one-third of the Gruyère and Parmesan cheeses over the garlic-sage layer. Repeat this procedure two times.

4. Dissolve the flour in the milk in a small bowl. Pour the milk mixture evenly over the top of the gratin and season with salt and pepper. Bake in the oven for 40 to 45 minutes, or until golden brown. Serve immediately.

Endive, Apple, Blue Cheese, and **Hickory Nut Salad**

Serves 2

Last winter at the farmers' market we found a vendor selling buttery hickory nuts. We bought a bag full and experimented with them. This salad was our favorite. Feel free to vary the type of apples. We like to use Gala or Jonathan because they are so sweet. Also, if you can find both the green and red Belgian endive, buy one of each to make an even more colorful salad.

2 Belgian endives, cut in half and thinly sliced
½ apple, thinly sliced
¼ cup crumbled blue cheese
3 tablespoons coarsely chopped hickory nuts

Vinaigrette

1 teaspoon Dijon mustard
3 tablespoons hazelnut oil
1 tablespoon white wine vinegar
Pinch of sugar
Salt and freshly ground black pepper, to taste

1. Place the endive and apple slices in a small salad bowl. Add the blue cheese and hickory nuts.

2. To make the vinaigrette: Combine all of the ingredients in a small bowl.

3. Dress the salad with the hazelnut vinaigrette, toss, and serve.

Stephen's **Cherry Biscotti**

Makes 16 biscotti

Biscotti have become almost as popular as bagels. We love the crunch of a crispy biscotti. They're especially delicious dipped in coffee, tea, or a dessert wine. This recipe, from Jessica's husband Stephen, includes dried cherries for a nice, unexpected surprise. The recipe makes more than is needed for serving two, but you'll be glad to have them around to enjoy with your morning coffee or as an afternoon snack.

2 large eggs
1 cup sugar
1 teaspoon baking powder
Pinch of salt
1½ teaspoons vanilla extract
2¼ cups all-purpose flour
½ cup finely chopped almonds
½ cup dried cherries, coarsely chopped

1. Preheat the oven to 350 degrees. Line a baking pan or baking sheet with parchment paper and set aside.

2. In the bowl of an electric mixer, beat the eggs on low speed until thick, about 3 to 4 minutes. Slowly add the sugar and beat until batter is a pale color. Add the baking powder, salt, and vanilla extract and beat until incorporated. Gradually add half of the flour. After the flour is incorporated, add all of the almonds and cherries, mixing by hand with a spoon. Add the remaining flour, still mixing by hand, until you can form the dough into a loose ball with floured hands.

3. Lightly dust the ball of dough with flour, divide the ball in half, and form each half into a log about 8 inches long. Place the logs in the baking pan and flatten them slightly so they are about 2½ inches wide.

4. Place the baking pan in the oven and bake for 25 to 30 minutes. Remove the pan from the oven and immediately transfer the logs to a cutting board. (You can do this easily by sliding the parchment onto the cutting board.) Let the logs cool so they will be easier to slice.

5. Using a sharp knife, cut each log crosswise into 8 pieces (not including the small end pieces), making diagonal slices every 1 inch. Spread the biscotti, cut sides down, on the baking sheet. Return the baking pan to the oven and bake for 10 to 12 minutes on each side, or until light golden.

6. Transfer the biscotti to a rack to cool completely before serving. Biscotti can be stored in a tightly sealed container or frozen in plastic bags for up to 1 month.

DINNER FOR 4

Bob's Classic Martini with Caperberries

•

Cheese Torta

•

Fennel Soup with Roasted Garlic Croutons

•

Bistro Skillet Steak with
Reduced Burgundy Sauce

•

Hot Potato and Frisee Salad

•

Caramelized Banana Bread Pudding

Menu Manager

Up to 1 day before dinner: **1.** Prepare Cheese Torta
2. Prepare Fennel Soup with Roasted Garlic Croutons and refrigerate. If Garlic Croutons are made in advance, keep them fresh in a plastic bag

Day of dinner: **1.** Prepare vinaigrette for Hot Potato and Frisee Salad
2. Prepare Caramelized Banana Bread Pudding

About 45 minutes before dinner: **1.** Bring steaks to room temperature

About 30 minutes before dinner: **1.** Boil potatoes for salad
2. Prepare Bistro Skillet Steak with Reduced Burgundy Sauce

Bob's **Classic Martini** with Caperberries

Serves 1

The martini has had a resurgence in popularity over the past several years. And it's no surprise. This classic cocktail has such a smooth, tangy taste and elegant appearance. Ellen's husband, Bob, adds caperberries, which we think makes the drink even more decorative and tasty. Its festive look and its warming effect are perfect at the end of a cold winter day. You can find caperberries at specialty food stores and occasionally at your local supermarket.

> *½ teaspoon dry vermouth*
> *2 ounces vodka*
> *1 to 2 caperberries*

1. Combine the vermouth and vodka with ice in a shaker. Shake several times and then strain the liquid through a fine-mesh strainer into a martini glass. Garnish with a caperberry or two and serve.

(Cheese Torta)

 Cheese **Torta**

Serves 4

The layers of cheese, pistachios, sun-dried tomatoes, and basil make this an aromatic, luscious, and colorful spread.

1 clove garlic
1 shallot
½ cup (1 stick) unsalted butter, at room temperature
1 (4-ounce) package Neufchâtel cheese, at room temperature
4 ounces goat cheese, crumbled
1 tablespoon dry vermouth
1 cup crumbled blue cheese
¼ cup chopped pistachio nuts
½ cup sun-dried tomatoes, soaked in hot water for 20 minutes to soften,
    drained and finely chopped
12 large fresh basil leaves, finely chopped, plus 1 whole leaf for garnish
Unsalted crackers or 1 baguette, thinly sliced

1. Using a food processor fitted with the metal blade, place the garlic and shallot in the feeder tube with the motor running. Process briefly to mince. Add the butter, Neufchâtel cheese, goat cheese, and vermouth, and process until smooth. Set aside.

2. Using a pastry brush, grease a 2-cup straight-sided mold or bowl with butter or oil. Line with plastic wrap, pushing the plastic into the corners and leaving about 2 inches overhanging at top.

3. Sprinkle half of the blue cheese, pistachios, sun-dried tomatoes, and basil over the bottom of the mold. Spread half of the butter mixture over the top. Repeat the layering with the remaining ingredients, finishing with the remaining butter mixture on top.

4. Fold the overhanging plastic wrap over the top. Refrigerate until firm, at least 1 hour.

5. To serve, invert mold onto a serving platter and remove the plastic. Garnish the top with the whole basil leaf. Serve with thinly sliced baguette or unsalted crackers.

Fennel Soup with Roasted Garlic Croutons

Serves 4

A slice of Italian bread spread with pureed garlic thickens this satisfying soup.

Roasted Garlic Croutons

1 head of garlic
1 teaspoon olive oil
4 (½-inch) slices Italian bread

Fennel Soup

2 medium fennel bulbs (about 2 pounds)

2 tablespoons olive oil
1 tablespoon unsalted butter
1 medium leek, cleaned and coarsely chopped
5 cups beef or chicken stock
    (preferably homemade)
Salt and freshly ground black pepper, to taste
¼ cup freshly grated Parmesan cheese

1. To prepare the Roasted Garlic Croutons: Preheat the oven to 400 degrees. Remove most of the papery outer skin of the garlic, but leave the head whole. Cut ½ inch off the top of the garlic head, drizzle with the 1 teaspoon olive oil and wrap in aluminum foil. Place in the oven and roast for 45 to 50 minutes, or until garlic is very soft.

2. During the last 10 minutes of roasting, place the bread on baking sheet in the oven and toast until slightly golden. Remove the bread from the oven and set aside.

3. When the garlic head is cool enough to handle, squeeze the garlic cloves out of the bulb into a small bowl. Mash the garlic with a fork and set aside.

4. To prepare the soup: Slice the fennel bulbs crosswise into thin slices. Heat the oil and butter in a large saucepan over medium-high heat. Add the fennel and leeks and sauté until softened, 5 to 7 minutes. Add the stock and bring to a boil. Reduce the heat and simmer, loosely covered, until the vegetables are very soft, 20 to 25 minutes.

5. Remove 1 cup of the vegetables and puree in a blender or a food processor. Stir the puree back into the soup and simmer just until heated through, 1 to 2 minutes. Season with salt and pepper.

6. Spread the toasted bread slices with the garlic puree. Place a piece of the toast in the bottom of each soup bowl. Ladle soup over the toast and sprinkle Parmesan cheese over the top and serve.

Bistro **Skillet Steak** with Reduced Burgundy Sauce

Serves 4

This bistro fare is warm, smoky, savory, and divine. We love this dish not only for its flavor, but also for its surprising simplicity. Increasing the sauce for larger groups increases the difficulty, so this is best when prepared for a dinner of four (or cut the recipe in half to serve two).

4 (6-ounce) sirloin steaks or
     2 (12-ounce) sirloin steaks, about 1 inch thick
1 tablespoon olive oil
½ teaspoon salt

Sauce

6 tablespoons beef stock
1 cup burgundy wine
3 tablespoons butter
Salt and freshly ground black pepper, to taste

1. Rub both sides of the meat with olive oil.

2. Dust a large cast-iron skillet with the salt. Preheat the skillet over medium-high heat for 1 to 2 minutes. Test the skillet's heat by sprinkling drops of water in it; when the drops sizzle and immediately evaporate, the pan is hot enough for the meat. Place the steaks on the skillet and cook until browned on the outside and red and juicy inside, about 3 to 4 minutes per side. Transfer to a warm platter.

3. Turn the heat down to medium. Add the beef stock to loosen the drippings and scrape them off the bottom of the skillet. Add the burgundy, stir, and cook for 3 to 4 minutes to reduce. The liquid should start to thicken as it gently bubbles. When the sauce has reduced, add the butter and cook until the butter has completely melted. Stir the sauce once, and season with salt and pepper.

4. Slice the steaks thinly, arrange on 4 plates, and serve with the burgundy sauce.

Hot Potato and Frisee **Salad**

Serves 4

This salad can be used with almost all of our menus. It is perfect served with meat or fish, and it goes beautifully with an omelet or a frittata for brunch.

3 medium heads of frisee
8 to 10 small red potatoes (16 to 18 if they are quarter-sized)
¼ medium red onion, thinly sliced
5 slices hickory-smoked bacon, optional

Vinaigrette

1 tablespoon whole-grain mustard
1 clove garlic, minced
Pinch of sugar
Salt and freshly ground black pepper, to taste
Juice of 1 lemon
4 tablespoons olive oil

1. Bring the potatoes to a boil in a medium saucepan over medium heat. Simmer for 15 minutes, or until a fork easily pierces their flesh.

2. Meanwhile, separate the leaves from the frisee, tearing off and discarding the bottom portion of the leaves. Place the frisee in a large salad bowl. Add the onion.

3. Place the bacon in a large frying pan or cast-iron skillet and cook until it is golden brown and crispy, 8 to 10 minutes. Drain on paper towels. When cooled, crumble into pieces and set aside.

4. To make the vinaigrette: In a medium bowl, combine the mustard, garlic, sugar, salt, and pepper, and mix it into a paste. Add the lemon juice and olive oil and whisk until creamy.

5. When the potatoes are tender, drain and cut the potatoes into quarters, or leave whole if they are small. Add the warm potatoes to the salad bowl. Whisk the dressing again and drizzle it over the salad. Toss several times to coat. Add the bacon and toss again. Serve immediately.

Caramelized Banana Bread **Pudding**

Serves 4

This recipe was inspired by Tim Fischer, manager of The Cook's Library. Tim is a talented pastry chef. He is generous with his knowledge and regularly brings in wonderful desserts for the staff and customers to enjoy. We always get sighs of satisfaction from our friends when we serve this. It is a perfect comfort food to share on a long cold winter night.

Softened butter, for coating baking dish

1¼ cups sugar

4 (1-inch) thick slices day-old bread, preferably challah (egg bread) or brioche, crusts trimmed and cut in 1-inch cubes

Caramelized Bananas

3 tablespoons butter

¾ cup sugar

3 ripe bananas, cut diagonally into ½-inch slices

1 tablespoon rum

4 tablespoons chopped pecans

Custard

2 large eggs

¾ cup whole milk

¾ cup heavy whipping cream

1 teaspoon vanilla extract

Confectioners' sugar, for dusting

1. Preheat the oven to 375 degree

2. Butter a 1-quart soufflé dish or other baking dish with at least 3-inch-high sides.

3. Melt the sugar in a large skillet or sauce pan, over medium heat. As the sugar melts, give it a gentle stir to make sure it has dissolved completely, and then leave it untouched until it becomes a golden color, 2 to 4 minutes, watching constantly as the sugar can burn quickly. Carefully pour the hot caramel into the buttered baking dish. Set aside.

4. To prepare the Caramelized Bananas: In a medium saucepan, melt the butter and sugar slowly, stirring often until mixture becomes a light brown. Put the bananas in the mixture and gently stir to coat and caramelize them. Remove from heat and stir in the rum and pecans. Set aside.

5. To make the Custard: Place all of the ingredients in the bowl of a food processor fitted with the metal blade and process until combined, about 30 seconds.

6. Spread half of the banana mixture, half of the custard, and half of the bread cubes on top of the caramel in the baking pan. Add the remaining banana mixture and the remaining bread cubes. Pour the remaining custard mixture over the top, pressing down so that all of the bread layers are soaked. Set aside for 10 minutes, until bread is moist.

7. Bake in the oven until puffed and brown, 50 to 60 minutes.

8. Sift confectioners' sugar over the top and serve warm.

6

Winter Sangria

◆

Fruity Fig and Black Olive Spread

◆

Winter Pot Roast with Juniper Berries

◆

Caramelized Root Vegetables

◆

*Chopped Winter Greens with Candied Pecans
and Honey Dressing*

◆

Fresh Gingery Gingerbread

Menu Manager

Up to 4 days before dinner: **1.** Prepare Cognac Ice Cream
2. Prepare candied pecans for salad if desired, and store in an airtight container

2 days before dinner: **1.** Marinate pot roast and refrigerate, turning several times

1 day before dinner: **1.** Prepare Winter Pot Roast with Juniper Berries, cool, slice, pour sauce over, and refrigerate
2. Prepare Fruity Fig and Black Olive Spread
3. Prepare Honey Dressing for salad
4. Prepare Fresh Gingery Gingerbread
5. Prepare Winter Sangria and let cool, but do not add fruit
6. Prepare vegetables for Caramelized Root Vegetables

About 90 minutes before serving: **1.** Bring pot roast to room temperature
2. Preheat oven to 425 degrees, cook vegetables, and set aside

About 1 hour before serving: **1.** Preheat oven to 350 degrees for pot roast
2. Add fruit to Winter Sangria and keep chilled
3. Prepare winter greens for salad
4. Remove root vegetables from refrigerator and set aside

About 45 minutes before serving: **1.** Put pot roast in preheated oven

About 15-20 minutes before serving: **1.** Reheat vegetables

At serving time: **1.** Toss winter greens with pecans and dressing for salad
2. Put Cognac Ice Cream in refrigerator to soften

 Winter **Sangria**

Serves 6

This sangria is named for all of the fall and winter fruits we add to the wine. The burgundy color and festiveness of the drink make it a perfect winter cocktail.

½ cup sugar
½ cup warm water
2 cups freshly squeezed orange juice
¼ cup freshly squeezed lime juice
¼ cup freshly squeezed lemon juice
1½ bottles red wine
2 tart apples (such as Granny Smith or Pippin), cored and quartered
2 Bosc pears, cored and cut into thin wedges
2 large navel oranges, halved and sliced into thin disks
1 lemon, halved and sliced into thin disks
1 lime, halved and sliced into thin disks
8 ounces red seedless grapes
2 cups club soda, chilled

1. Combine the sugar and warm water in a small bowl. Let the syrup stand, allowing the sugar to melt.

2. Meanwhile, in a large bowl, combine the orange, lime, and lemon juices with the red wine. Stir in the sugar syrup and refrigerate the mixture for at least 1 hour.

3. Add the apples, pears, oranges, lemon and lime slices, and grapes and stir. Just before serving, add the club soda. Serve in tall glasses over ice.

Fruity Fig and Black Olive Spread

Serves 6

This unusual salty-sweet Mediterranean spread is delicious served on toasted baguette slices with a glass of sangria or full-bodied red wine.

4 dried or fresh figs
¼ cup plus 1 tablespoon port
2 tablespoons drained capers
3 anchovy fillets, chopped
2 tablespoons olive oil
2 cups pitted Niçoise olives
Juice of ½ lemon
2 tablespoons finely chopped fresh basil
Freshly ground black pepper, to taste

1. If you use dried figs, soak them in the ¼ cup port for 1 hour, or until soft.

2. Combine the capers, anchovies, and olive oil in a food processor or a blender until blended. Add the olives, figs, lemon juice, and the 1 tablespoon port and pulse the mixture 8 to 10 times until blended. Add 1 tablespoon of the basil and pulse again.

3. Spoon the spread into a small serving bowl. Garnish with the remaining basil and the freshly ground black pepper.

Winter **Pot Roast** with Juniper Berries

Serves 6

This homey dish is the perfect size for six to share. Be sure to marinate the meat for at least several hours, or preferably overnight. We recommend cooking the pot roast the day before your dinner, so remember to begin two days before your dinner, with a night for marinating and then a day to cook the meat. The day of the dinner, all you have to do is put it in the oven to reheat. The juniper berries give the roast an extra zing.

Marinade

4 cloves garlic
1 cup Cabernet Sauvignon or other dry red wine
4 small sprigs of parsley
2 teaspoons freshly squeezed lemon juice
Several small pieces lemon zest
20 juniper berries, crushed
Freshly ground black pepper, to taste

2½ to 3 pounds chuck or rump roast
2 tablespoons olive oil
1 tablespoon unsalted butter
½ cup finely chopped onion
1½ cups Cabernet Sauvignon
1 cup beef stock, or more if needed

1. To make the marinade: Combine all of the marinade ingredients in a shallow bowl.

2. Add meat to marinade. Place in refrigerator, turning the meat 2 to 3 times. Marinate several hours, or overnight.

124

3. Remove the meat from marinade and reserve marinade. Dry the beef carefully with paper towels so it will brown and make delicious brown bits on the bottom of the pan. In a Dutch oven or a heavy casserole large enough to hold the roast, heat the oil and butter until sizzling. Brown the roast well on all sides, 10 to 20 minutes. Remove roast, set aside, and add the onions. Sauté onions until soft. Add the marinade and scrape up all the brown bits on the bottom of the pan. Bring to a slow simmer.

4. Put the browned roast back in the pot. Cover with a lid and cook at a low simmer for 1½ to 2½ hours for a flat roast, 2 to 3 hours for a thicker roast. Turn the roast every 20 to 30 minutes during cooking. After the first hour, check liquid. Keep about ½ to ¾ cup of liquid in the pan. The roast should be tender when a fork is inserted. If it is not tender, cook longer.

5. Remove roast from the pan. Deglaze the pan with ¾ to 1 cup of the wine. Add about 1 cup of beef broth and cook until thickened. There should be about 1 cup or more of reduced sauce. Taste and adjust for seasoning.

6. Cut the meat in thick slices. Place slices in an ovenproof casserole. Pour the reduced sauce over the slices and refrigerate, covered, overnight.

7. To serve, preheat the oven to 350 degrees. Remove the meat from refrigerator and let it come to room temperature, 30 to 45 minutes. Heat in the oven for 30 to 45 minutes.

Caramelized **Root Vegetables**

Serves 6

These vegetables are sticky and sweet and complement any roast or stew. There are so many wonderful root vegetables to choose from; feel free to use sweet potatoes, parsnips, rutabagas, celery root, or fennel as alternatives.

5 turnips
4 medium Yukon Gold potatoes, quartered
8 small red potatoes (cut in half if larger than a golf ball)
6 carrots, cut into thirds
8 shallots
2 tablespoons olive oil
2 tablespoons balsamic vinegar
Salt and freshly ground black pepper, to taste

1. Preheat the oven to 425 degrees.

2. If the turnips are older, the skin could be thick and fibrous, so it is best to peel off about ⅛ inch of the turnip, enough to get to the meat of the vegetable. If the turnip is younger, just scrub it like the other vegetables. Cut the turnips in quarters.

3. Put the turnips, potatoes, carrots, and shallots in a large bowl and toss with the olive oil, balsamic vinegar, salt, and pepper. Transfer the coated vegetables to a medium roasting pan. Bake in the oven for 45 to 50 minutes, or until golden brown. Check for doneness by piercing the vegetables with a fork; if the fork enters the vegetables easily, they are done.

Chopped **Winter Greens** with Candied Pecans and Honey Dressing

Serves 6

You'll be surprised at how varied the tastes are in this salad. The greens range from bitter to peppery, and the pecans add a salty sweetness.

Candied Pecans

2 tablespoons butter

6 tablespoons brown sugar

2 tablespoons water

½ teaspoon salt

1 cup pecan halves

Dressing

1 teaspoon Dijon mustard

1 tablespoon freshly squeezed orange juice

1 teaspoon freshly squeezed lemon juice

1 teaspoon freshly squeezed lemon juice

3 to 4 tablespoons honey

2 teaspoons sherry vinegar

⅛ teaspoon salt

⅛ teaspoon freshly ground black pepper

6 tablespoons olive oil

2 small escarole, finely chopped

1 bunch mustard greens, finely chopped

2 curly endives, halved, cored, and finely chopped

1 head of radicchio, halved and finely chopped

1. Preheat the oven to 300 degrees. Line a baking sheet with aluminum foil. In a medium saucepan, combine the butter, sugar, water, and salt. Add the pecans and stir to coat. Spread the nuts evenly on the baking sheet and bake in the oven for 30 minutes, turning every 10 to 12 minutes.

2. Meanwhile, whisk the Dijon mustard, orange juice, lemon juice, honey, sherry vinegar, salt, and pepper together in a small bowl. Whisk in the olive oil.

3. Remove the nuts from the oven and set them aside to cool for 15 minutes. Put the cooled nuts and salad greens in a large bowl. Add the dressing, toss thoroughly, and serve.

Fresh Gingery **Gingerbread**

Serves 6

The inspiration for this recipe came from an old community cookbook Ellen found. We've added a lot of fresh and candied ginger to give it more spice. Serve with fresh whipped cream or Cognac or Cinnamon Ice Cream (page 55).

Butter and flour for coating pan
½ cup sugar
½ cup unsalted butter, melted
1 cup molasses
1 large egg
2½ cups sifted all-purpose flour
1½ teaspoons baking soda
½ teaspoon salt

1 tablespoon ground ginger
1½ teaspoons ground cinnamon
½ teaspoon ground cloves
½ teaspoon freshly grated nutmeg
1 cup boiling water
2 tablespoons freshly grated ginger
⅛ to ¼ cup candied ginger, finely chopped

1. Preheat the oven to 375 degrees. Butter and flour an 8-inch square or round baking pan.

2. Combine the sugar, butter, molasses, and egg in a medium bowl and beat well.

3. Sift flour, baking soda, salt, ginger, cinnamon, cloves, and nutmeg together into a medium bowl. Stir this mixture into the egg mixture. Stir in the boiling water. Add the fresh and candied ginger.

4. Pour the batter into the prepared pan and bake for 25 to 35 minutes. The cake is done when the sides pull away from the edge and a knife inserted in the center of the cake comes out clean.

5. Remove the cake from the oven and let cool in the pan for 15 minutes. Remove the cake from the pan and finish cooling on a wire rack.

6. Serve cake on individual plates with fresh whipped cream.

Index

Table of Equivalents

The exact equivalents in the following tables have been rounded for convenience.

Liquid and Dry Measures

U.S.	Metric
1/4 teaspoon	1.25 milliliters
1/2 teaspoon	2.5 milliliters
1 teaspoon	5 milliliters
1 tablespoon (3 teaspoons)	15 milliliters
1 fluid ounce (2 tablespoons)	30 milliliters
1/4 cup	60 milliliters
1/3 cup	80 milliliters
1 cup	240 milliliters
1 pint (2 cups)	480 milliliters
1 quart (4 cups, 32 ounces)	960 milliliters
1 gallon (4 quarts)	3.84 liters
1 ounce (by weight)	28 grams
1 pound	454 grams
2.2 pounds	1 kilogram

Length Measures

U.S.	Metric
1/8 inch	3 millimeters
1/4 inch	6 millimeters
1/2 inch	12 millimeters
1 inch	2.5 centimeters

Oven Temperatures

Fahrenheit	Celsius	Gas
250	120	1/2
275	140	1
300	150	2
325	160	3
350	180	4
375	190	5
400	200	6
425	220	7
450	230	8
475	240	9
500	260	10